Our Hearts Come Home For *Christmas*

Betty Lowrey

ISBN 979-8-9919162-0-2 (paperback)
ISBN 979-8-9919162-1-9 (eBook)

C h a p t e r   1

Derek's 2ⁿᵈ Grade

Jeff Larson gave the sign a cursory glance that morning as he drove out of town. Mosby. Population 1001. "Make that one thousand even," he said, tipping his cap. He had enough. Jennie hadn't come home last night. He had taken little Dereck to school, shoved a five dollar bill in his hand, pressed a kiss on his forehead and said, "If I'm not here when school lets out, call your aunt Nell."

Dereck's big eyes took in the suitcase in the next seat, his father wearing his Sunday clothes and their stop at the gas station to fill up the car. "You going somewhere, Dad?" His father was silent. "What about work, Dad?" His Dad acted as though he was hunting something in the glove compartment. When he put that kiss on his forehead, he knew he was on to something. "Bye, Dad."

"Bye, Dereck. If I'm not here when school lets out, call Grampa or Aunt Nell." His dad pulled away from the drop-off curb. Dereck waited but his dad didn't look back.

Dereck glanced around the school's play yard. It was bare as a baby's butt. That was a phrase he'd heard Grampa say. "Whose baby?" He used to ask but after all the times Grampa laughed he'd finally figured it out. There was no baby and sometimes it meant the apple tree hadn't bore an apple.

1

Things were changing. Uncle Harry left Aunt Nell. She came home to Grampa. They hadn't seen hide nor hair of him since, according to Grampa. And there wasn't hide nor hair of anyone on the play ground this morning. Dereck shift the book bag on his back and walked through the double doors, into the hallowed halls of Mosby Elementary.

Catrine and Lindy Stevens were standing where the hall made an L toward the second grade class rooms. They smiled and waved, starting toward Dereck but he cut through a group as if they didn't exist and avoided the girls. They managed to come up from the rear, "If you're looking for

Elizabeth," they broke into laughter. "She's sick. You won't find her here today." They hopped around in front of him, walking backwards down the hall so they could face him. "You shouldn't let her build that big old snow man, Dereck. Her mother sent a note to Miss Murphy saying she has a sore throat and running a fever of 103. I guess no matter where you live you can get sick."

7th Grade

"That was some snow storm. I wish we had another." Derek came into the room as Junior Hawkins elaborated on the snow. "It was knee deep and Dad made me feed the dogs. You got boots, he said."

The girls looked up as Dereck entered. "Your girlfriend's sick." They showed no remorse. "You shouldn't been out in that snow, Dereck. Now she can't be at school and if not at school can't cheer the game." So that was their happiness. Elizabeth was the one who called the cheers and they resented her.

Bobby Dugan came by his side, jabbing a finger against his chest. "Yeah, man. You made her sick. It's all your fault, just like in second grade. Remember that?"

"May be my fault but you're the one said, let me get the shovel and, we can rake the snow up faster and you did."

Bobby laughed, bringing Dereck down onto the floor in a head-lock. Dereck was not happy. If they got caught, it was him would feel the teacher's wrath. Bobby was like a celebrity around school.

"Miss Patrick's coming," Catrine warned. "Get up now. Stop, Bobby. Let him up."

"Aww, she ain't gonna do nuthin. Wait and see."

Sure enough, Miss Patrick stopped to talk with Bobby but she ignored the others, Dereck included.

"You look pretty, today, Miss Patrick. But you always do," Bobby exclaimed. "How do you do that?"

"Why thank you, Bobby." Miss Patrick patted the pocket of her jacket. That's where she kept her cell phone. Then she turned to study Dereck. "Well, Derek Larson, don't you look flushed. You're not coming to school with a fever are you?" The room got deadly quiet. Everyone was waiting to hear her plow into Dereck. "You better not come In to my room with a fever. I'd have to talk to your Grandfather, if you did." Everyone knew Derek Larson had neither parent around, just his Grandfather.

"Yes, Ma'am, Miss Patrick." Dereck stammered his reply and sank an inch or two lower in the seat.

"I can't have sick children in my class room, like I cannot tolerate wrestling in the halls. Now, you boys would never do that would you?" Her eyes pierced their soul.

"No, Ma'am, Miss Patrick." They said in unison. "We won't."

"Good."

Catrin's hand was waving wildly in the air. "But Miss Patrick, they were…"

Miss Patrick's attention was drawn to Catrin. "They were innocent bystanders? That's what you are trying to tell me, Catrin?" Miss

Patrick smiled. "We are putting the whole thing to rest, right now. I appreciate all of your attention. Now, let's get down to today's business. We are going to have a wonderful day." Catrin's hand went down as she straightened in her seat. Miss Patrick won this one. Or, did she? Catrin's hand was up, once more, her shoulders squared.

"Yes, Catrin?"

"Poor Elizabeth is sick with a cold since she and Dereck and Bobby made the snow man yesterday."

"Yes, I received a note from Elizabeth's mother. Remember? I shared that information with you, earlier. Thank you, Catrin." She paused a moment and then said, "They build a snowman every year. According to Miss Murphy, this has been going on since they began first grade." She smiled at Catrin as if to say, too bad you weren't invited to join them. She saw Catrin turn to give Derek an evil eye.

****

Patting the covers, Nancy Ann leaned across the pink chenille spread of Lizzie's bed. Nose to nose looking into Lizzie's, she said, "I know I shouldn't have let you stay out yesterday. I'm so sorry you have this old cold. I wish you'd let me take you to the doctor this morning."

"I'll be fine, Mommie. I don't think it was being outside yesterday, but the piano recital last Sunday. Mrs. Hon kept hovering around us, tweaking everything, patting our shoulders, but when she wanted to put a bow in my hair, I just ran. Anyway she had a cold and coughed all over us. Wouldn't you think she would know to keep a kleen-ex handy?"

"I don't know which is the worst, out in the snow or someone coughing."

Elizabeth was indignant. "Germs, Mother. Germs."

"Remember that when you date some old boy and he wants to kiss you," Nancy Ann replied, "Honest to goodness, you out there yesterday with two boys building that snowman. Don't you have any girl friends?" Mentally she noticed Elizabeth change from calling her Mommie, a sign of caution.

"I do, but you can't trust them. They want everything you have and I am growing up."

"Surely not. You're only a baby." Nancy Ann gave a deep sigh. "You girls are trying to grow up too fast."

"I'm not a baby, Mother, we're at a standstill; Nowhere to go and nothing to do here."

"I heartily disagree, you keep me on the road. I never knew I'd be a chauffeur." Nancy Ann walked to the window peering out on the frozen ground. "I hope you daddy gets home before too long."

Elizabeth hoped so, too. He had been stranded in St. Louis all week and she missed him.

"Go to sleep, Honey. Daddy should be here in the morning."

****

Elizabeth didn't remember when she drift off. Once she thought she heard the doorbell and then soft crying. But she couldn't come out of the dream she was having and sank into deeper sleep.

Again, she heard voices. They were not happy voices. In the dark, she climbed from the bed and made it to the door, her ear against the crack, wishing she could open it further. Sobbing. She heard sobbing, it was her mother sobbing and speaking in a broken almost guttural voice. She listened. Who was with her?

"How could you do this? All these years you've stayed in touch with her? All the lies. All the years I've made you look good to my friends, to the community. All the years I asked why didn't we move to the big city and you said "No, Elizabeth needs the wholesome life a small community offers? You lied to me, to her, to our community that has taken you into everything, the church, serving on the bank's board," Suddenly her sobs turned to wild hysterical laughter, not a pleasing laugh, a desperate half sob, half cry for help. "You bastard. You bastard."

Elizabeth opened the door a bit wider, peering down the stairs to see her parents standing in front of the fireplace; it's embers a dying glow, an occasional flicker on their face, in an otherwise dark room.

"Shh," her father cautioned, a hand reaching to touch her mother. "Shh don't waken Lizzie."

"Don't touch me." Nancy Ann rounded Frank like a crazed cat stalking prey. "You care whether she sleeps or not? You fear for her sleep when tomorrow her world ends."

"Her world doesn't end, it changes."

"It ends."

"Says who?" Frank Turner peered into his wife's face. "I say we go on as usual. I come and go."

"I say it ends. You see that woman again and I swear by God in Heaven, the Creator of my life, I will take Elizabeth and leave this town and you will never see her again."

"You would do that, to me, to her? When you know how much I love her?"

"Apparently not enough to keep your goods in your pants, and I'll see that she never forgives you for that."

"We can't help who we love, Nancy Ann."

"What was that you whispered in my ear twelve years ago, Frank? Remember me? We walked down the aisle together and you promised 'til death do we part. I'm not dead yet, Frank." She was screaming now. Frank gave a hurried glance toward the upper stairs, and grabbed her quickly his hand over her mouth, holding her until she slumped against his body.

"I didn't mean to. It just happened." For a minute his body seemed to buckle and then straighten. "How did you find out?"

"Evidently you have an enemy. The doorbell rang and when I answered no one was there but a letter was stuck in the storm door handle. I noticed it when it fell but whoever left it was gone."

"Then you know the rest."

"Yes." Nancy Ann turned toward the stairs. "You have the sofa, Frank. I don't want you in my room."

Hurriedly, Elizabeth closed the door and ran back to bed. She was on her side, one arm over her head when her mother came to lay a hand on her forehead, and seeming satisfied turned and left.

What was the rest, Elizabeth wondered. What more was to be added to Daddy's story? They were supposed to have guest the next night, would they come? Elizabeth hoped not. She would see to it, with fever.

****

Elizabeth watched Catrin rummaging through her jewelry drawer. She had hoped the Collier's wouldn't come but here they were, their daughter in her room picking through her drawer. It didn't seem to matter when Nancy Ann Turner walked in. "Why Catrin, what are you doing in that drawer?"

"I could show Elizabeth how to straighten this drawer, Mrs. Turner but she says she don't feel up to it.

She says she's running temperature. I felt of her head and it feels normal to me."

Elizabeth eyes sent darts flying as her mother turned to leave. "There's nothing normal about you going through my things. I prefer you don't."

Catrin flopped on the opposite twin bed. "I like the way your mother decorates. My room's pale blue, a boy's Color. Daddy says my mother should hire your mother to redecorate but mother doesn't like another female in her house. It's probably best as my mother doesn't need to be around your family too much. She thinks your daddy looks like George Clooney, probably has an…you know, an attraction to him. Just my opinion."

"You have a lot of opinions." Elizabeth flopped on the bed, all but covering her face with the sheet.

Catrin turned to study Elizabeth. "Has anyone told you, no I don't imagine they have, Derek Larson was my partner for the May Dance practice?" She picked a piece of fuzz off her dress. "Since you were gone and we didn't know but what you had strep and would be out for days. Practice must go on."

"Who would make them think I would be out for days? It's a cold and I had temperature one day."

"Well, I'm bored. If you're not sick get up and show me what you do in this God forsaken house when you're here." She laughed. "I nearly gag when your mother elaborates calling it Safe Haven." She did the sign, acting as though she stuck her finger down her throat. "What kind of name is that?"

"Why would you call my home God forsaken?"

"Everybody knows the story." An evil gleam was in Catrin's eyes, as she flopped on the bed by Elizabeth, staring almost nose to nose into her face. "Did you think it was a secret? Your daddy has a mistress in the city. Rumo*r says they are having a child.*" She waved one dainty finger in the air. "I guess you won't inherit this big ole mausoleum all by Yourself, now, will you?"

"Who cares?" Elizabeth braced herself. That stung. She guessed that was the rest of daddy's story. How could you go down and have a meal and act happy after those words? All she could do was refuse to go down for dinner with Catrin and her parents, let her own fend for themselves.

"Then let's talk about other more important things. You missed school today and the try-out for cheerleading is tomorrow. That means you can't be there, according to the rules if you aren't present the day before you can't participate in school activities that occur the following day." She stood up to act out one of the last cheers. "That means I have a chance not only making it but maybe being Captain of our team."

"All's fair in love and war." Elizabeth swung her feet over the edge of the bed. "I believe it's time we go down."

"In your pajamas?"

"Oh, I forgot. I'll just be a minute." She disappeared inside the closet to emerge five minutes later fully dressed.

Catrin was sitting cross legged on her bed reading her diary. "Hmmm," she said, "I suppose Darquin is Derek." She laughed, 'You do make your writing interesting calling people by names other than their own and the witch is that me?" Catrin laughed, "That is simply delicious, because I know how you feel about me. And aren't you over dressed?"

Elizabeth took the diary from Catrin and closed it. "Your mother will love it."

Sybil Collier was speaking as they joined the group. "It's just so refreshing, Nancy Ann, to find friends like you and Frank and our children be compatible." She clapped her hands. "Elizabeth you look darling."

"But we aren't," Catrin announced, "Compatible. We compete on every level. Just think what the next ears of our life will bring."

Nancy Ann was studying Catrin. "I declare, Sybil," she said, "Your daughter does seem much older for her age than mine."

Sybil laughed. "You need to turn yours loose more, Nancy Ann. I declare, with Frank gone you all live a sheltered life. Of course, you must worry about that, too, him the spittin' image of George Clooney."

Boyd came in on the last of the conversation, laying an arm around his wife's shoulder. "It's a good life here in Mosby. I know Frank just lives for the day he can leave that city business and come back here full time." He turned to Frank, "You know there's a need for an attorney here in Mosby."

****

Tenth Grade

"We get to help with this year's prom. Aren't you excited?" Cat was busy examining herself in the cracked mirror.

Elizabeth had other things on her mind. "Should I be excited to serve those upper class snobs who look down on us?"

"Why would you say that?" She watched Elizabeth pulling the zipper up to her jeans. "P.E. is just a hindrance."

"Catrin Collier, that's what you said last week when I told you it was discussed we might have to serve at the prom."

"Well, that was last week, this week Lawrence Hendrick winked at me in study hall. He is so dreamy.

Wicked, too."

"That wicked bothers me a little, hmmm? Wonder what he did to get that attached to his name." Elizabeth studied Cat. "You haven't learned a thing have you? If your Daddy ever finds out about that little drinking spree you and James Fenmor had under the bridge last weekend; I do not want to be within hollering distance."

Cat giggled. "It was worth it. I wish you hadn't pulled me out of there when you did. I might have learned something."

"I think…you are learning enough on your own without the senior boys." They were headed to their lockers.

"You can't talk. Derek's as old as they are because his parents kept him out of school until he came here to live with his Grampa."

"The difference being, his mother ran off with someone, his daddy left and right here in town, well, his granddad did make him go to school and that's the best thing happened to him. He learns well and he wants to learn, so that's different."

"I know lots of people look down on him because of what his mother and daddy did. Why does your mother look the other way?" Cat watched Elizabeth trying to open the door to her locker, finally to kick the bottom and it sprang loose.

"Excuse me. I don't understand the question."

"Well, like my mother, your mother is considered crème of the crop here in Mosby and they don't associate with the Underlings. Heaven forbid." Cat threw her dirty clothes into the locker. "I'll be glad when this day is over and we can go home to our snobbish parents…oh, I forgot, you only have one parent at home. Your Dad escapes to the city."

"Yeah, he does. I doubt he would if his business wasn't there."

"At least you got a lawyer in the family if you need him. Dad sets great store by your daddy."

Elizabeth turned to face Cat. "Oh, yeah, why is that?"

Cat shrugged. "He doesn't elaborate but why not? I like your dad, don't you?"

They stared at each other, thinking back, not daring bring that subject around.

******

"Did you see this?" Elizabeth held the paper in front of Catrin, "A list of rules as long as a sheet of paper. What do they think we are going to do? We are servers with trays in our hands or glasses of beverage being refilled." Shaking her head she started down the hall. "It's mandatory we have to serve at the prom, or I'd back out. Our name on the line was just a curtesy."

"Why does it bother you? I need you there, to cover for me when I duck out with Lawrence." Cat giggled. "He says there's a closet just outside the door where they store supplies. It's being cleaned out this week due to the Prom."

"Ugh. I can imagine the smell." Elizabeth tapped the paper. "It says right here, No Leaving the Ball Room."

Cat's giggles were infectious, "Ballroom? All I know is there's a gymnasium and then there's the closet for kissing." She made a grand gesture, "But if they want to call it the Ball Room. Okay."

"Promise me you will be careful. I can't cover for you the rest of my life. You're going to get me in trouble."

"Spoil sport. What can happen in a closet?"

"Depends how large the closet is, I suppose."

****

Twelfth Grade

"Why aren't you and Catrin friends anymore?' Sybil paused with the coffee cup midair, waiting for Elizabeth to answer. "You don't have to keep it to yourself; her mother called me and said it's your fault."

"Of course she would say that!"

"What happened?"

"I don't want to talk about it." Elizabeth waited for the toast to pop up. "Why is this thing slow?"

"It has a few years on it. You'll be slow when you get a few on you."

"You're not."

"We're not dropping this conversation. Does it have to do with Derek Larson?"

"Is that what Sybil Collier said?"

"It is her opinion he is interested in her daughter." Nancy Ann's eyebrows lift as Elizabeth laughed. "I take it that is not your opinion?"

"Mother, I have spent twelve years with Catrin undermining everything I do. Now, I've finally realized it's not worth it, I don't give a damn and I'm not doing it anymore."

"Where did you learn to curse?" Nancy Ann rose up from her chair at the table. "Usually when two women have a falling out there's a man hiding behind one of their skirts. Is Derek hiding?"

"No. If you must know, I was chosen for the Basketball team's candidate for Queen. Catrin came in second and that didn't set well. She raised such a stink they're letting her march too, because her daddy is on the school board and they are the richest family in town to call on when the school needs something…so guess who she whines and puts up another stink to march with?"

"I'm assuming Derek. That's not right."

"Right isn't always right, is it Mother?' The toaster popped making them both jump. "I never heard of a school inventing a queen of honor before, but that's her title and it shouldn't have been her right to choose Derek and she has only done it to insult me, further. There's one last meeting to decide it."

"How does Derek feel about this?"

"He refused to march with her."

"How did that go over?"

"Coach told him if he didn't march with Catrin he doesn't play that night." Elizabeth placed the toast on a plate, added butter and jam and carried it to the table as her mother sit back down. "You want to know the reason Coach stood with Catrin and the sponsor allowing this whole mess?" Nancy Ann Fay nodded. "The Colliers are sponsoring the mats and safety gear for the new wrestling program."

"It's always money, isn't it?"

"Catrin used to think we had money, us living here in your mother's house and it being almost as large as theirs, of course she always wanted you to come decorate theirs, just as her daddy did, too."

"I didn't know that."

"Yeah, but Sybil won't allow another woman in her house, their help is all male."

"So, what is Derek going to do?"

"What can he do? His grant would be at stake, next. That's how school politics works."

"Want me to try to do anything to even this out?"

"No, I want to live above their rules, and then I have nothing to worry about."

"Smart girl."

"Somehow that doesn't bring much comfort."

"So who will you march with?"

"Bobby Dugan."

"He seems like a nice enough young man but I wouldn't want you marrying either one."

"I'll give that some consideration."

Chapter 2

Coach Worley was angry. No, it was more than that, he was downright mad.

"What do you mean, Larson can't play the game. If he doesn't play we lose."

"Then you need to tell him to put his muzzle on and mind what we tell him. He's marching, Let's rephrase that, "he's escorting Miss Catrin Clippard, the daughter of the richest donor to our sports program, the one who has funded all the safety gear for all programs. Did you Understand that? I said ALL." Superintendent Myers pointed to a chair beside his desk. "Sit." He waited for Coach to unwind his feet and settle his elbows on the chair arms. "Now, listen Up. You get this shit in order or you will be out of a job come next year, maybe before. Our School needs this win. Larson needs this win because there are scouts coming tonight to Watch him play. Guess who set that up? The mighty Boyd Collier has contacts. He did it."

Coach pushed back so quick his chair went flying against the wall as he stood. "Politics. That's all this is. One snot nosed rich kid doesn't get her way and Daddy steps in."

"Sad to say, you're right. Politics got you a job, mine and every other teacher in this school. It's where we live. I hear tell of other schools, they don't go through what we do, but here, we have to jump through all the hoops and make things happen, that's how we have the highest paid salaries."

"We're just a hick town in the boonies. How does that happen?"

"It happened when we got our act together and hired a dumb ass coach eight years ago that led us to Victory eight years in a row and a bunch of rich daddy's decided they liked the fame and they'd chip in and give the school the best if the teachers talents were sifted through a sieve to their liking which means their kids have a chance at the best twelve years of education a kid can get. Did you think our rating happened by luck?" He could see Coach's anger was turning to some thing else. "Let me approach this a different direction. I understand through the grapevine you just purchased a house and further than that there's another baby on the way to that house."

"That's personal and no one's business."

"No, that's common knowledge. Those same rich daddy's keep tabs on their investment."

"Are you threatening me?"

"No, I'm just telling you it behooves you to explain to Derek Larson he has to commit to this game tonight in order to keep the grant he already knows is coming his way and for you to keep your Job. It just so happens every one of those rich daddy's serves the school board and Boyd Collier Just happens to be the President of the School Board, but you knew that."

Coach walked to the door, placed his hand on the door knob and turned to look at Myers. "Do you mind telling me what happened to the last coach? I've only been here three years."

"You don't want to know."

****

"Listen, Derek, you have to march with Catrin Collier. They will take whatever scholarship you have and make your graduating year a miserable mess." Coach's voice rang across the gym's bleachers.

"Did you stand up for me?"

"I did but I got put in my place, too. I was sweatin' by the time I left that office. I shouldn't be sayin' this front of a student, but I didn't realize so much hinged on what the atheletic department does. It seems the rich daddy's have control of the school board, the Superintendent and unknownst to me, my job too."

"What you are saying is that my marching with Catrin makes everyone happy."

"You got it."

"I'll do it." Derek rose off the bench. "But I will not promise I'll dance every dance with her, after the game." He was half way to the door when he turned and ask, "What were you going to do if I said no?"

"I was going to ask you to do it for me, so I wouldn't get fired. We have a baby coming soon."

"Okay." Derek left, wondering how Elizabeth would take the news. She had counted on him.

****

He barely had time to finish wiping the wax off Grampa's old truck.

"You go ahead and get ready. Your uniform's laying on your bed. I'll finish this for you. I don't want Elizabeth having to wait for you."

"It's not Elizabeth I'm marching with, Grampa. They switched it on us today at school. I have to escort Catrin Collier."

"Hmph. Mighta known Boyd's family would come in on this, they do everything else." He turned to stare at his grandson. "You want to talk about it?"

"No, I don't have time."

"What'd Elizabeth say?"

"That it wasn't the end of the world."

"She's right."

******

It wasn't the end of the world but Catrin wouldn't turn loose of him long enough to dance once with Elizabeth. He spoke with her, when Catrin went to the rest room.

"I thought she would never go," he said when he finally found Elizabeth sitting alone at one of the tables. By the look on her face she wasn't enjoying the dance either. Bobby was in a huddle with three other guys and who knew what they were doing? "You still think it's not the end of the world?"

"No, it's not but I thought we would get to dance a few dances but Cat does seem to monopolize you."

"There's still the Prom," he said, hopeful. "Will you go with me?"

"Yes." A smile popped up, and she looked forgiving for once. "I'll wait for you when this is over."

"Elizabeth?"

"Yes."

"You know I have to take her home, don't you?"

"Yep"

"I'll be right back then."

"You do that." She sounded relieved. "I'll be at the Oak."

That was even better. Now to get rid of Catrin.

"But the dance is not over," Catrin whined. "I want to stay to the end. Come on, let's dance."

Not wanting to appear he was being coerced, Derek followed her onto the floor. When the dance ended he said, "Catrin, I escorted you according to Coach and the team. I attended the victory dance with you but now…I am going home, with or without seeing you to yours. What do you want to do?"

"I had someone watch while I left you for ten minutes. I know this is all because of Elizabeth, isn't it?" He shrugged and walked away. "Oh, crap, wait up, I'll go with you. Don't make me look ridiculous."

"Only you could do that." He opened the truck door for her, waited until she pulled the giant skirt of the dress inside and shut it against her whining reply.

****

He parked Grampa's truck, ran inside and changed clothes, grabbed the radio and left again on his bicycle before Grampa turned the light on in his bed room. He had left a note. That was all that was needed. The oak was at the edge of Turner property, or as the town folks called it Mosby Acre.

She was there, sitting on the bench they'd made together from wood left over from one of Nancy Ann's projects. He sit beside her. She had brought a light throw of some kind and handed him a corner to pull across his body, locking them beneath its warmth. The city lights cast just enough of a glow on them.

"Well, that was some offering they demanded. I don't know if I feel honored or cursed. That girl talks all the time. No, let me rephrase that, she whines."

Elizabeth chuckled. "Just do whatever you have to to keep her from claiming you for the prom."

"You mean the coach, the school board and her daddy. Who knew I'd play a part in the scheme of things."

"Have you ever been to the Collier's home?"

Derek shuddered. "No, is there something spectacular about the place? May the Lord forbid that requirement of me." When she didn't reply he turned to study her face. "What's there?"

"I don't know, except it seems strange that Cat's mother has all male help and they are always there."

"Is her daddy?"

"Actually he is, anytime I've been…but anymore that's not a lot. Catrin seems bent on causing me problems."

"She's jealous."

"Of what?"

"Just who you are."

"But she has everything."

"Well." He reached for her hand. "She wants more. Whatever you have, that's what she wants."

"I hope you are kidding."

"I'm not." He gave a troubled sigh. "This is our last of everything we've known, Elizabeth. Then we will graduate, have our last summer and have to say goodbye as we go different ways to college."

"I know."

"Wish I didn't have to go, but there's no future for me if I don't."

"I know."

"Listen to you, girl. Almost twelve years of school completed and you know two words." She giggled.

"I brought the radio. We didn't send off and get a piece of junk, you know, we have a real live emergency radio that picks up one station and will help to protect us if we ever have a war on U. S. soil."

He went to the bicycle for the little radio with its wire attached and hung it from the tree.

Pulling her up, he said, "I've waited for this dance all night." The only light was the street lamps in the distance but they were enough he could see her face. "You were the most beautiful girl at the dance."

"If that were true, not a lot of good it did me. I couldn't even snatch a beau." He pulled her close.

"You snagged one now. Besides, I paid all those old boys to stay away from you. I'm broke."

"Guess you'll have to get a job then." He let her slide away to the music and back into his arms, "Any suggestions?"

She laughed. "I'm going to help mother's upholstery lady. She said she needs a care giver. I ask her what for and she said to bring some comfort to her soul because everything's falling apart around her."

"Can she afford two people? I mean, we couldn't. Grampa works at home in that little old shed out back, sometimes, and then if he's able there's always someone wanting him to lay carpet but that's the reason he cut his work load. Laying carpet, down on your knees wears the knees out." The music stopped and they sit back on the bench. "So there won't be any money made if I don't find a job."

"Try Margie. There's no telling what she will ask of you. Remember, her husband has been gone four years now and she has had to work in the upholstery shop, meaning maintenance has been void."

"Gone? As in left or died?" Derek thought of his own situation, when his dad left and mother before that.

"I'm sorry. I know what you're thinking. It was by death. Her husband died."

"Elizabeth?"

"Yes."

"Thank you for never looking down on me."

"Derek…I wouldn't."

"I know, but some people do, I always knew that, even in fifth grade."

"You have made your own way. People respect you and love you."

"Do you love me, Elizabeth?"

The sound of the remaining leaves rustled on the trees. Time stood still.

"You've never asked me that before. I always assumed you knew I do."

"Then say it."

All the words of her mother washed over Elizabeth. "I…ah…I… guess I'm embarrassed."

"It's not that hard. Here, I'll say it. We will graduate, come May. I love you. Now, Elizabeth, do you love me? I need to know. I have a future to plan and I want to know if you are part of it."

"Yes." Her voice was soft, so soft it was lost in the traffic of last minute couple's leaving the Dance. He was holding her hand, squeezing for dear life. "Derek, I said yes." She began to laugh, a nervous sounding laugh, as he whooped and threw his arms up in the air, first, and then grabbed her.

"Nothing makes me happier. I had to hear you say it. The whole evening Catrin has filled my ears with complete nonsense, saying you were just using me for a boyfriend, in word only, when we went our separate ways you would forget all about me because you think you're too good for me."

"Why would she do that?"

Derek shrugged. "Why does Catrin do any of the things she does? She knows all my family left me."

"Trust me. Catrin doesn't know who I am, or who we are, I will never leave you. We will complete our college degree and locate in some place that helps us take care of each other. We have to decide right now, whether we trust each other to last that long"

"I want to tell you something Elizabeth. All my people in life have left me. I would be so hurt if you gave up on me and left me." His voice was as sad as his expression. She couldn't stand it. And then he said, "I'm afraid it would tear up my world in a way I can't even explain."

She couldn't resist, "I suppose then you would get really mad at me?"

"I don't even want to imagine it."

****

The weather next day was anything but normal. The morning brought wind lashing at the trees, limbs falling and lawns littered as though it were March, when the area reminded people of tornado alley.

The radio warned people to stay in. It was the kind of atmosphere where anything could happen.

The newspaper proclaimed another victory for Mosby Basketball team and the fact that Derek Larson was being asked to play basketball at Macomb located in Illinois. "Why so far away," Nancy Ann asked, secretly glad of the distance. "I thought maybe near us, the Cape or the Bluff." Her daughter's sniffles were enough she quit thinking out loud. "He will come home, Sweetheart."

"Don't pretend you aren't glad, Mother. If possible you would have paid to have him far away from me." Elizabeth wiped the tears from her cheeks with the back side of her hand. "He can't come home except on holidays, Easter, Christmas and maybe Thanksgiving." Her phone dinged and she read the new text out loud.

"Guess where I've decided to attend College. Isn't it just a hoot that it's where Derek will be going?

"Who is that from, Elizabeth?"

"Who do you think, Mother? It's from Catrin."

The wind picked up, moaning around the corners of the house. Nancy Ann built a fire and sat near the hearth absorbing the heat. She wished Frank was home, but then he probably was with his other family. Glancing at their daughter she wondered if they were wrong to keep so much from her, but if she knew they hadn't known what she might do.

Elizabeth turned on the television. "Did you hear that, Mother? They said we have a tornado not three miles from here and they are listing it as EF4, isn't that severe?"

"Yes, it is. Let's get in the closet. It has a better support system. I think we're in the quiet period before the storm. Do you hear it in the distance?" Elizabeth shook her head, but in only minutes it was there.

They heard the onslaught and felt it as well, as the house shook from the force of wind. The tornado was moving fast. Within minutes it had passed and they came out of the closet to go outside to access the damage. "Thank the good Lord, here the damage seems minor with only trees down."

The next morning brought concern. Roofs had been taken from the high school buildings and already the school board was meeting. Mosby residents were out on the streets cleaning away the debris.

By Monday morning it had been decided the next day they would begin bussing the grades nine through twelve into the city.

"This first day is to give you a day to find your way around," Superintendent Meyer said. "There's a burger place across from the High School and you will have to go there for lunch or wait until we return to Mosby." It was at noon when they went across the road to the Burger Place it happened.

****

Elizabeth heard Catrin's lilting voice, "Why Mr. Turner, is your office nearby? We're going to be coming here until they get the roofs replaced at our school in Mosby." Making a quick turn, Elizabeth darted into the rest room. She'd seen the woman sitting opposite her father and she could not face them. Derek had turned to stone it seemed and was backing up to the counter but he could still hear the conversation.

"Hello Catrin," Elizabeth's father replied. "This is my secretary."

He didn't want Mr. Turner to see him. Quickly, he turned toward the restrooms ducking down behind a low wall to wait for Elizabeth. When she didn't come out for over a half hour he determined he would call her out and put his best effort into calling her name as he found her book bag with her purse in it tossed aside, knowing just how terribly upset she was with her father. Her eyes were red when she came out. He handed Elizabeth her purse as he whispered, "Follow me. I've been here before, and there's a glen of trees not too far that hides a small stream of water. We can wait out the lunch hour."

She didn't question. She followed.

"Do you know what this is about?" Once they were seated she studied his face for reaction.

"No, I don't."

"Do you remember fifth grade when you and Bobby and me made the snow man and I got a cold and was out of school for the whole week?" Derek nodded. "Well, I was never sure if it was for real or a dream…I heard my parents quarrelling and my mother told my dad if he saw that woman again she would take me away and he would never see us again.”

“Based on his having lunch with his secretary, how can you be sure now that it was real?”

“I feel it. Here.” She touched where her heart would be. “You heard Catrin. Now she’ll spread…”

“Are you worried more what Catrin does or that there’s a possibility of something else?”

“Both, but Catrin will cause people to stare at me and talk behind my back and it all hurts.”

****

When they returned to Mosby, Derek was one of the first to get off the bus. Catrin was fast, plopping down in the seat beside Elizabeth. “You didn’t speak to your father, did you?” She waited for Elizabeth’s reply but there was none coming. “I know why. Remember way back? Years ago?

I told you your daddy has a mistress and I said there was rumor she had his child.” She turned to face Elizabeth.

Catrin seemed in charge of the situation and Elizabeth was in such shock she couldn’t think.

“I did hear she lost that child. It seems your father is full of indiscretion.”

“All these years…is that why you’ve been so cruel, without me knowing why you were holding this over my head?”

Mortified, Elizabeth set through the inquisition, wondering where it was leading. “I’m not telling what I know, anyway, could be I’ll need you to stand up for me some day, so my lips are sealed.”

Not knowing how to take this side she’d never seen of Catrin, Elizabeth remained quiet.

"I…uh," Elizabeth didn't lift her head. "I don't know anything about any of it."

"Don't worry about me. I may need something from you, soon." Catrin stood to navigate the aisle.

****

Life was not the same after that day. Elizabeth didn't discuss it with her mother but for some strange reason she felt her mother knew. Nancy Ann seemed to clamp down Elizabeth's movement within the community. Eventually her father returned home.

Frank came to her room, knocking on the door. "Are you all right? You've hardly left your room."

Elizabeth nodded seeing her father peep around the door. "I'm okay."

"Your mother tells me it's settled where you will attend college." Again, she nodded. "How about Derek, did his scholarship go through? No? Well, it will. The school may be using it to whip students into compliance with their new rules. Not you, of course, but those who question everything."

"I don't see how one individual's scholarship could be used in such an unnecessary manner."

"True. But people use everything against people these days. Shall we talk about what Catrin saw?"

He eased down onto the bed by her, both their feet at an angle on the floor. "I have to tell you the truth of the matter, Lizzie. Five or so years ago, I did something I'm not proud of, I had an affair."

"I don't know if I want to hear this Dad."

She emotionally moved away from her father, she had to have a clear head. He was not leaving.

"Are you still involved with her?"

"No, I'm not. Your mother said if I was she would take you away where I couldn't see you, much less find you. I couldn't have that, Lizzie. I'd die if I couldn't come home to you and mom."

"But you were with her…" She saw her father's sadness and yet, he had betrayed her and Mom.

The hurt was flooding her mind, body, soul. "I gotta go, Dad." She left him sitting on the pink spread.

She had to go to the treehouse they'd built, her and Derek. A second group had their eye on it, but it was theirs, they'd built it from the best of everything they could find. Maybe life said you join clubs knowing one day you would give it all up because of age, but sometimes there was trauma. So who cared if they were graduating this year? The tree house was still on her parent's property.

She had been there only minutes when Derek joined her, sitting beside her as usual on the bench.

"I thought I'd find you here." He studied her face a moment. "What's happened? Tell me."

"My dad told me he'd had an affair. He said it's over but if it is, why was he with her?" A tear lipped from the corner of her eye and with his thumb, Derek wiped it away.

"It's not the first time someone had an affair, Elizabeth, and it's not the end of the world."

"Not for you."

"Nor you. We will make a life of our own together and it will never happen to us."

Her words were preceded by a choked sob. "Don't they say never say never?" Her shoulders shook as she tried to control the flow of tears but they burst out, a strangled cry as his arm went around her.

"It feels like the end of the world. I noticed he wasn't coming home as often and Mother has been different, almost secretive and now I understand why."

"Your mother doesn't like me. She barred me from your twelfth birthday party, I've always known."

"It's not you; she is afraid I'll make a mistake and have to live with it the rest of my life."

"Am I a mistake, Elizabeth? A little boy whose parents both left him, grown up and ready for college because I've tried to overcome those things…and I've tried hard to impress your mother but she never bends."

"Maybe because my Dad betrayed her and she's not having anyone else do the same."

"Look at me." He placed a hand on each shoulder and turned her to face him. "Do you think I would betray you? I love you."

"Today…I don't know. I never thought my Dad capable of such a thing."

"Why didn't you ask him? For heaven's sakes, Elizabeth, you had a chance, maybe there's circumstance."

She jumped to her feet, shouting, "No, Derek, there's never circumstance to betray your wife and daughter. Get that out of your mind. I won't accept it. Never." She started walking away. He was behind her. She began running and ran until her breath gave out and would have fallen to the ground except he was there, breathing hard, and he caught her; his arms around her, tight as a band.

"You can't run from me, Lizzie."

"Don't call me that. My Dad calls me that…when"

Derek cut her off, "When you're upset?" A gentle laugh followed his words. "That's who you become, hurt and bewildered and it just sounds right. Lizzie." He nuzzled behind her ear. "You seem to become someone we want to protect. I want to protect you from hurt, Elizabeth. I have to go off to college, learn something and be a man. Then, when I have a job, we can get married. Say yes,

Elizabeth." His hold on her loosened as he tilt her face to meet his eyes and waited for the answer.

"Say yes. That's all I'll have to keep me going while I'm that far away from you."

"You will find someone else," she replied bitterly. "That's what men do."

"I am totally wiped out. You ran like hell. I thought I wasn't going to catch you."

"You don't curse." She sounded so indignant; it caught them both by surprise. She began to laugh first. "I did that the other day and my mother ask me where I learned to curse." He stopped laughing.

"The occasion seemed to call for it." He rubbed his ribs where the laughter seemed to have settled.

"I don't. Gramps wouldn't allow it."

'I like your Grand dad."

"Oh, yeah? Then maybe you'll like me." A grin spread across his face. "I believe I just ask you to marry me and if that's not suitable, to please wait for me…forever…a lifetime…eternity, maybe?"

She held up on hand. "Stop. I'll wait."

"But you didn't say yes."

"That comes after all the other things you mentioned, college, a job…forever, a lifetime, eternity."

"At least you're smiling." He did a mock throw at an invisible basket. "I'd say that will do for now."

******

They made it through the Senior year of high school. Time to graduate arrived. Catrin pouted, fumed and stomped her dainty foot. This time, the coach who was over-seeing the line-up, went chin to chin with her. "Catrin Collier," he was near shouting. "I won't do it. Go home tell your Momma, your daddy and the Sheriff if you want, or straighten up and act like the young lady God in heaven intended. If there's one thing I believe, it's this, if Derek Larson asked to march with Elizabeth Turner, then he will. What the school board has put me and him through this year, I will not budge. So zip it."

Within thirty minutes Sybil Collier dressed in her best, five inch heels and breathing fire descended upon the gymnasium where they were practicing. She marched straight to the coach.

"Evening, Mrs. Collier," the coach greeted her. "Are you here to give assistance with this deserving group of graduating students? How nice. Now, we have a little problem and we are trying to be very fair about it." He gave his best raw-bone smile. "By the way, when you graduated from Mosby High, were you allowed to march with someone you really wanted to march with? Tell us about it."

Flabbergasted, Sybil glanced toward the seniors, lined up and ready for practice, even Catrin. "Well, it was an exciting event, and well, Boyd and I were dating, in fact we became serious about dating each other that week end, anyways…we marched together because we were dating."

"I am relieved you shared with us, Mrs. Collier, we are experiencing whether to follow the same type of procedure. I believe your daughter has an idea whether we should or not. Is that why you are here?"

Sybil looked her daughter square in the eye. "What do you think, Catrin. Yes or no?" Mother and daughter were aware all Catrin's peers were listening intently, the silence was strong as they waited. Neither batted an eye. The silence grew until finally Catrin spoke.

"Yes, I believe that's what they all want. Thanks, Mom."

Catrin walked out of the gymnasium leaving her mother standing looking quite perturbed.

Elizabeth thought of her own mother. For two months her father had not come home and then he was back but he didn't circulate in the community and she wasn't sure her parents slept together. Either her mother was the strongest or the most stubborn. She hadn't decided which. Theirs was a community where everyone knew, or thought they knew your business. There were nosey questions, "what's happening with Frank, haven't seen him in a while." Catrin seemed to always be within hearing distance and would give Elizabeth a knowing look. Elizabeth tried to avoid her but like a bad penny, Catrin was there, whether watching reaction from Elizabeth or keeping tabs on Derek, again, Elizabeth wasn't sure.

****

That summer Elizabeth and Derek worked together helping in the Upholstery Shop. Sweating and busy they would say at the end of their free time, it was the best ever. Margie was easy to work with. She had hired two young people willing to work. The bonus was as large as she could afford, "but it's no match for you two in what you've done to help me," she said.

It was nearing time for Derek to leave to get settled before the classes began. He had been following A pre-arranged strengthening schedule with the coach after work each day and Coach assured him he would be ahead of the other team mates.

"I'm going into a whole new world, Elizabeth. You won't be there, or Gramps and I will face all kinds of new things. What if I can't do it? Nothing will be familiar."

"That's when you will grow, Derek and four years will fly by. I wish I could be there to see you play."

"Will you watch the games on t.v.?" He shuffled, embarrassed, "I mean the ones I'm allowed in."

She hugged him. "You will be great. Just don't get caught up in Catrin's sneakiness. I can just see her plotting to tie up with you and if that doesn't work she will parade every friend she has by you."

He picked her up and swung her around. "You don't ever have to worry about that." She was shaking her head vigorously when he sit her down abruptly and placed his hands on each side of her head, bringing their lips together. "What did you tell me? Four years is not a lifetime, forever or eternity." Now he studied her face. "Are you still thinking you can accomplish what you need in three years? Run that eternity thing by me again."

She began to laugh. "I think you have that completely out of context. You ask me if I'd wait for you four years, forever, eternity." He was grinning. "You set that one up didn't you?"

One evening she heard her father on the phone. Whatever was being said left him distressed. He asked her mother to take a ride with him and when they returned Nancy Ann had been crying. Her father went upstairs to return within the hour carrying two suitcases. He kissed her cheek and promised to explain soon. "Something's come up, Lizzie. I have to go. I'll talk to you later."

"What's happening?" She asked but her mother refused to comment.

"Not now, darling. I can't go into your father's leaving. He has to tell you himself."

"If it's the affair, he told me he gave her up. It's your fault, isn't it? You won't take him back."

"You have no idea what you're talking about." Nancy Ann locked herself in her room.

They navigated the halls of the big old house, sad eyed and miserable and then Derek left for college. Elizabeth would follow in two weeks, but for now she continued daily to help Margie who clucked over her like an old hen.

****

She cried for a week after Derek left. Her mother said, "Be active, Darling, don't let that childish infatuation you have for Derek Larson ruin your life." Elizabeth was putting the last suit case in.

"Why would you talk to me about Derek? I want to know why my father left. Now I don't know if he will meet me half way, like he said, to say good bye." She started the car, ready to drive off.

"Of course he did." Nancy Ann turned away. "No one has considered who is going to be alone, here, have they?" The old sadness claimed her for a moment. "You will be happy. Your father is happy."

Bitterness welled up in Elizabeth. "You could forgive him and what does it take, Mother, letting him back in your bed?"

Nancy Ann retorted, "You have absolutely no idea how it feels to be rejected, your life turned upside down, to know the one you loved with all your heart made love with another woman when we had promised to love each other til death do we part." She held her daughter's gaze. "It hurts, Elizabeth. It's a pain you never put down. You talk about forgiveness? One day something will happen. I pray not this. But something will happen and you will remember this conversation. Your father said he would come home to see you, with you gone he will not continue to come home to me. Think on that."

Elizabeth was ten miles down the road before her mind settled to consider her mother's words. So that's what it was, he had lied to her. He lied to both of them. No, he probably wouldn't come home to his wife when he was making a new life in the city.

Three Years Later

She was busy with study when the phone rang. She was expecting a call from Derek and rushed to pick up the cell.

"Elizabeth?"

"Yes."

"It's Dad."

"I know."

"Honey, I'm in your vicinity and I would like to take you to dinner and have you meet someone."

"Is she with you?" Hostility sounded in her voice. "I'm not interested Dad. I have a mother."

"It's your brother, Elizabeth. He's two years old, harmless but a lot of fun. I might add extremely intelligent and talks better than most two year olds. We don't know where he gets his vocabulary." He was quiet for a minute before he added, "Sometimes he lapses into a normal toddler's talk, forgetting verbs or linking words. We think it's psychological."

"Now why would he do that?"

He ignored the question. "Peppercorn's on Village Square if you haven't been there. Thirty minutes."

The line went dead and she was standing as still as a statue with the phone in her hand. Trying to gather her thoughts she glanced at the clock on the wall. He gave her just enough time to get there. She stepped into her shoes, and walked out of the apartment, six blocks to the restaurant.

He came from a far table when he saw her enter. "You came." His voice was full of relief.

"I have always respected your wishes, though the last year has been a struggle."

"From your point of view, I'm sure it has. But I was there for you eighteen years of your life."

"And now I'm supposed to understand you have to give someone else their share of what was mine?"

"That's one way of saying it. Follow me. I've ordered what you normally choose. Is that all right?"

"I'm not really hungry, anyway. It's fine." She followed him to the table where a child sit.

"Elizabeth, this is T.J., your brother. T.J., this is the wonderful person I told you about. Elizabeth, your sister." He could have been a mannequin, she stared at him a cookie cutter image of her dad.

T.J. stared at her, his brown eyes wide with curiosity, but his mouth in a straight line, and no smile.

"My mother said you might not like me."

Elizabeth sat across from him. "Don't you think we should let that be solved by both of us? We don't know whether you will like me."

"I want to." His shoulders seemed to slump. "My aunt's children aren't allowed to play with me."

"Really? That's too bad." With a glance to her father she saw him raise one eyebrow as his mouth went into an I can't help it form. "Well, since this is our first time meeting, let's see what we think."

Dinner was a forced issue. T.J. ate his macaroni and cheese and drank the glass of milk. She and her father mostly twiddled the fork in their hand. Finished, J. T. scooted back in his chair and watched her.

"Do you work?" She asked him. "I mean you are on a business trip with your dad."

A grin played at the corners of his lips. "No, I just asked if could come with him this trip." He slipped down from the chair and came across to put his hands on her shoulder, implying she must lean toward him. He whispered, "I didn't think he would let me but he did and Momma said be a good boy."

She waited until he climbed back onto his chair. "And have you been a good boy? Because, I didn't know the rules to travel with your dad, so I'm glad you have told me. I have to be good. Right?" While she ignored her father, T.J. nodded vigorously. Before he answered, T.J. was down from the chair and pulling her closer to his level as he whispered in her ear.

"Would you like to go fishing? We are going fishing tomorrow and you can go, too, but you have to bait your own pole." His voice was as solemn as a church preacher and then his eyes lit up. "We're getting those long creepy worms. Daddy says fish love them. I can't wait." His face transformed into a wreath of smiles. "You want to go?"

"No, I can't." The smile dimmed on T.J.'s face. "Your mother should go. You'll have fun."

His face crumbled. "She can't. She's sick." He went to stand by Frank. "It's bad. She's going to die."

Elizabeth turned to her father as Frank took the child's hand in his. "Is that true?" Frank nodded.

"Should you tell that to a child his age?" She wanted to ask him, was this woman pregnant with your child all those years back when our home was invaded by someone or something that tore our family apart and if so, as Catrin seemed to know did she lose that child and now here's a replacement. But she didn't. Instead, she repeated, "should you tell that to a child?"

"His mother told him. She feels he needs to be prepared." He saw her disapproval. "She has stage four cancer, Lizzie. She can't last." He gave a troubled sigh. "That's one reason I'm still with her." He spread his hands wide. "How could I abandon them, Lizzie? She had it when she gave birth to T.J. It's a miracle she lived."

Elizabeth felt nauseated, all the times she'd felt resentment toward her father and still the bitterness swallowed her reasoning and filled her heart with pain. He wanted to do good and could only choose one place in which to do it and he chose his son. But, her mind reasoned she was older, the child had to have someone if he lost his mother. It wasn't fair, but she was finding life wasn't fair.

"Let's get out of here." She saw her dad lay money on the table, but she was far ahead and pushed through the doors, out into the world of fresh air and space, space to turn loose of the horrible truth, but she couldn't. Before she could gather her thoughts, T.J. reached for her hand.

"You're sad." His own eyes filled with tears. "I cry when Mommie cries. Then we snuggle up and she takes a nap."

His tears created something she didn't want inside of her. God was saying you have to love him and she was resisting, all the while seeing her father waiting, waiting for her reaction. If she touched either of them, she would bend to what they wanted. She would not touch either of them. "I've got to go." T.J. was pulling on her hand, trying to pull her down. She leaned without thinking the consequence.

Bony little arms went around her neck. "Let me kiss you," he said. "you won't be sad." She felt his kiss on her cheek and knew he was waiting for her to do the same. God help me, she thought. Help me not to give in to this. It's wrong. She stood straight. I have a mother back home and she's alone because of him. T.J. wrapped his arm around her leg. "I can't reach you. I kiss your leg."

Through muffled sob and mixed laughter, she reached down and lifted him up. "Why you are light as a feather," she said. He laughed and wrapped his arms around her neck so tight she couldn't breathe.

And then he leaned back and looked into her eyes.

"Your eyes like mine. I like your eyes. I don't like my eyes. They're not like Momma's."

"So you think we have eyes alike?"

"Like Daddy's?" He was studying their father's face. "Like Daddy's. One, two, three."

"Three eyes, huh."

"No silly. One, two, three. Me, you, Daddy." And he gave her another kiss. His laughter bubbled up and she found herself laughing with him.

"You're the silly boy. What are you laughing about."

"I happy." But the smile receded and sadness came across like a shadow. "Momma don't laugh."

He heard Elizabeth say she was sorry. "Can you come home with me?" She shook her head no.

"Can you fish with me and Daddy?" Her hesitation was not lost. "Please," he said. "Please."

Without thinking she kissed his cheek and handed him over to her dad. "I gotta go, T.J. Bye."

She walked away without kissing her dad goodbye. She might break if she kissed him.

She heard him call, "Seven thirty in the morning, Lizzie. We'll be by. Seven thirty." She kept walking.

Derek called that night. After a few minutes he asked, "What's wrong Elizabeth?"

"Nothing." She couldn't share something that was tearing her up inside. Not yet. "Just kind of blue.

It's the weekend and nothing to do. Except watch your game on t.v., I guess."

She watched Derek's game, waited for his call after and went to bed, still gloomy and still remembering little arms around her neck. She tried to put the kisses on her cheek aside and tried to sleep. Finally, the next morning, feeling at odds with the world, she pulled on a pair of old jeans and a sweat shirt, going out on the street to run. It was six thirty when she began the run and seven fifteen when she returned to the apartment. She was still sitting on the bench outside the complex when she heard a horn honking and looked up to see her dad and T.J., waving wildly her direction.

"You ready?" Her dad asked, as the car pulled in front of where she sit. His face was wreathed in smile. "You need a hat. It may be fall but it's going to be hot out there." T.J. was jumping up and down, clapping his hands.

"I'll be right back." She ran up the steps, grabbed a straw hat from the coat rack and locked the door as she left. Returning, she climbed in the back with T.J. Instantly he reached across to claim her hand.

****

Soon all hooks were baited and in the water. T.J., sitting watching his pole for something to bite.

"I would like for you to meet T.J.'s mother." Frank cast out into the water and waited for her answer.

"Why?" Confusement shown in her eyes. "I've met T.J., now, but I don't think I can handle that."

Great sadness shown in his eyes. "She's dying, Lizzie and she wants to know if you will be there for T.J.?"

"That's not necessary. You will be there." She stepped back as if stepping away from his request.

"I'm not sure."

"What?" She thought he would laugh and say," just joking", instead his lips tightened and his brow furrowed with lines.

"I don't know how to say this. Of course your mother doesn't know. I have a large tumor growing Inside of me, they've not decided yet, what can be done. They're thinking radiation will be tricky."

"You are waiting this late to tell me…surely you knew?"

"No, I honestly didn't. So much has gone on. All the turmoil. T.J. Your mother kicking me out."

"You chose, Dad. You chose and look where it got us all." Bitterness turned the words sour.

"That's all in the past, now, Lizzie. I need you to step up to the plate. This is your brother and he has no one else."

"Surely his mother has family. What's her name? His mother?"

"Sarah. She has no family. She was an orphan trained by the state in secretarial skills. That's how she came to be my secretary." He watched Elizabeth's eyes dull with hurt, followed by anger. "I am sorry."

"Sometimes, Dad, I don't think you are. You aren't the man that was my father when I was a child. Now I'm grown and you don't seem to know what to do about me since you have your son."

His shoulders slumped. "I love you both."

"But allowing yourself to love her is what made the problem. You already had a wife to love and I know she loved you. Now I watch her growing older, listless and alone, because she doesn't know what to do with herself."

"I know."

"No, you don't because you have another family and now you tell me there's a problem I'm supposed to fix" She sighed and then watched as T.J. pulled in a fish. "Yay. T.J., look at you." She ignored her father's expression as he was still dealing with her words. "I hurt inside, Dad, that you have cancer and that T.J.'s mother is dying. I haven't had time to think it over and I don't know what I'm supposed to say…but today, right now let's put it aside and get through this day so we can the next one."

****

Three days later the phone rang. "Hello, Darling, it's your mother."

She had just come in from running. After classes all day she found herself unable to sleep if she didn't do something to rid the tension. The park was easy access with its running track across the street.

"I know your voice, Mother."

"I rode up with Margie. She has a meeting and I wondered if we could have dinner together?"

"Only if you don't keep me out too long, I have a test tomorrow."

"I promise. I just want to see you."

****

They had ordered. Elizabeth felt there was more to come. "Why are you really here, Mother?"

"The grapevine is busy in Mosby. I think Catrin has been talking. Has she quit college?"

"I don't know. Remember? We are no longer friends. I don't know or care what Catrin does."

"It has to do with your father. She has a tale going around town that he is terminally ill. Is he?"

"Why would you ask me?"

"Because no matter how unfaithful he is as a husband he has always been a good daddy to you."

"But I don't keep tabs on him." Elizabeth picked up the menu left by the third place setting.

"No, but he does you and I have a feeling you know." She reached for Elizabeth's hand. "Look at me.

Is your father ill?"

"Why would you care?"

"I loved him, Elizabeth. Perhaps a part of me still does, although we will never be together again."

"It's his wife that's ill. She is dying."

Relief shown on Nancy Ann's face. "I'm glad it's not him…that sounds heartless but then it's just that…"

"She has your man," Elizabeth finished the sentence. "Don't feel too relieved. He does have a problem. The doctor's found a tumor…"

"Is it serious?"

"Yes." She watched her mother's expression change to one of sadness.

"The doctor wants to send him for another opinion, in case they've missed something."

"Sybil's not my friend, I know that," Nancy Ann began, "But she said his whore lost the baby five years ago, or was it six?" She grimaced. "Oh, these damn feelings I…you'd think it would be over; my feelings for him." She dabbed her eyes with the cloth napkin. "I'm sorry, that's the only time I curse, when I think of them together and Sybil knowing and Catrin anxious to tell everything to anyone that listens."

"There was a time you would have kept me home for a week if I called someone a whore."

"Your older now. Grown up enough to understand how a woman hurts when someone takes her husband." She lay the napkin back on the table, took a deep breath and continued. "I can do this."

******

Two hours later Elizabeth was tossing and turning in her bed. The terrible truth was if something happened to her father and T.J.'s mother the child would be alone. He was just a little boy. "You eyes like mine." His words resounded in her head. She needed to sleep. Tomorrow's test…please, God she prayed let me sleep but whether it was God or her own conscience she didn't sleep and couldn't study either. "You eyes…" What was the reason a child who didn't know the full scope of his father and mother's relation-ship would have a psychological problem that revealed its self in the way he talked?

What could Catrin possibly know or tell people about her fam-ily and why? Why wasn't she at school? Her relationship with Derek was having its own struggle; dating long distance was not easy. She missed too many of his calls and when she watched his games she saw the way the cheerleaders fawned over him. The jealousy she felt in the beginning was waning to a sad acceptance. Sometimes she felt caught in a time warp she had neither created or knew how to solve. She tried to pray about it all, and found herself falling asleep mid-prayer, nothing petitioned and no prayers answered.

****

It was two days until the winter break. Five o'clock in the morning her cell rang. She glanced quickly at the clock. She needed that last hour of sleep. Last night she was up late cramming for a test.

"Hello."

"Elizabeth, it's Dad. Can you come?"

"Where?"

"To the hospital. Sarah's dying. T.J. is here with me. If you could come for him and take him home?"

"They allowed a two year old in the hospital with his mother dying?" She was in shock.

"Don't question, Lizzie. Can you come for him before it happens?"

"Yes, of course. It will be probably twenty minutes before I arrive."

****

"Your father said to bring you in," the nurse said. "Come this way. Your little brother is so sad."

They were unhooking lines, leaving only the oxygen connected to T.J.'s mother. Feeling awkward and as though she were invading private territory, she accepted T.J. into her arms as her father stepped again to Sarah's bedside. She edged toward the door, but turned when her father spoke.

"Sarah, you wanted to meet Elizabeth?" There was a faint wiggle of one of Sarah's fingers. "Come closer, her father said and as she did he placed his arm around her shoulder drawing her in. "Sarah, this is Elizabeth."

Elizabeth looked down on the fragility of the woman, dark hair damp around her face. She saw the ravage of disease had not taken away the beauty of the woman. Dark lashes fringed eyes that examined and questioned. Recognition dawned in her eyes even as her breathing sound throughout the room and the nurse who was standing outside the door stepped back in. T. J.'s arms clasp Elizabeth's neck, in tiredness his head settling on her shoulder.

"Hello, Sarah." Elizabeth's voice was faint in her own ears.

"Love my baby." It was a whisper. Sarah's eyes pleaded and her fingers beckoned.

Elizabeth hesitated. "She wants to touch you, Lizzie." For a moment she glanced at her father.

Holding firmly to T.J. Elizabeth reached through the bed rail. She did not hear the words but saw Sarah's lips move. "Thank you." Seeing tears were building in Sarah's eyes, Elizabeth felt intense pain wash over her. She had not known T.J.'s mother was only a few years older. Did her mother know?

Later, as she sit, trying to gain control of the rush of feelings she could not put down, T.J., sound asleep in her arms, she could not contain the wash of thought battering her mind. Her father, twice as old as the woman who gave birth to his son, her father…supposed to be an honorable man in the community where they lived…her father who had shamed their very lives. She was at a loss how to handle it as she sit in a public hospital knowing as surely as she lived the little boy in her arms any moment would be a motherless child and his father grieving. How could she face the enormity of a tragic situation she had not caused? Anger, confusion and unacceptable but prevalent was the stark reality of sadness she had seen and felt in the woman's eyes. It was too much. She glanced down at the piece of paper her father had pushed into her hand; the address where they lived. Now she checked the time on her cell. She had been sitting there two hours holding a sleeping child.

******

She heard her father weeping. It was two in the morning according to her cell phone. She tried to get comfortable on the twin bed six feet away from where T.J. lay. She had found pajamas and swapped them for his day clothes; all the while he remained asleep. Now his mother had died. What would happen to him? Could her father work and see to his care? Evidently he had been active in some part of his life these last two years because he had been very scarce for three in hers.

Restrained, considering her thoughts, she did not go to him. How had hours passed and T.J. slept through them and how had she? Tomorrow she would call the college to find the alternatives. All class requirements were completed but would they allow her to miss again. The haunting eyes of Sarah's portrait on the wall behind T.J.'s bed was watching her.

She arose as usual at six thirty, thinking he would be asleep but found him clean shaven in the dining room at a desk strewn with papers. She stood, waiting, until he felt her presence.

"Come," he pointed to a chair beside the desk. "Thank you for bringing T.J, home last night or was it yesterday?" A film seemed to pass over his eyes. "Sarah passed shortly after you left but it took hours for the rest of…." His voice slipped away. "For them to come for her body."

"What will you do now?"

His hand passed over the desk top. "She had a burial contract, she said she took out years back thinking there would be no one to bury her. She insisted I find it. Maybe I've skimmed over it and not recognized it. She said it has the name Hamilton marked on it….she said this on the way to the hospital.

She knew she wasn't coming back." He leaned forward, propping his head in his hands. "I'm sorry, it just seems so unreal…she took care of everything here in the house…I just went to work each day."

"Have you slept at all?"

"No, I couldn't. I showered and shaved and dressed, but then I didn't know what to do, so I have been looking for the envelope." He leaned back in the chair, obviously tired and at loose ends. "Do you want to look?"

"I can. Why don't you sit over there in that recliner? I'll take your chair, here."

He seemed relived someone would tell him what to do. "Thank you for bringing T.J. home."

"Dad, you said that already. He has been asleep since we left the hospital."

"He has to absorb it all. It's traumatic for a little boy."

She was silent remembering it was traumatic for a grown daughter. She went through the stack of envelopes on the side first and then began with the pile he had strewn across the desk. It was when she heard his breathing smooth into a pattern she glanced over to see he had fallen asleep in the recliner. We all need comforting by someone that cares, she thought, realizing she did care. Right now, the man Sybil Collier considered handsome as a well-known movie star appeared old and tired and needed rest. She found an envelope marked Hamilton stuck between two large manila folders and laid it aside.

She made the call to the College, explained the situation and was given leniency to stay with family. She penned a note to her father and was ready to leave when T.J., padded into the dining room.

"Momma holds me." His whisper not to wake their father was louder than his speaking voice.

Putting her finger to her lips, she let him follow her into the next room where she settled onto the sofa. "You can rock me," he said. "In that chair." She removed her jacket and settled into the rocker as he crawled up on her lap. "Is my Momma here?" She pulled him closer to her body. "She's not, is she?" Elizabeth felt his body tremble and glanced down at his face. Tears ran down his cheeks. "I love my Momma."

"I know." She soothed. "I love my momma, too."

She didn't keep track of time. This seemed to be what she should be doing as T.J. slipped back into sleep and she wondered that she had not known her father was living in the same town. Why would he do that?

"I dreamed of Momma." She came out of the deep fog of trying to sort things out to see T.J.'s expression. "Look, Lizzie, I happy. Momma said be a big boy and be good. She has to go but she will be back." He reached up to hug Elizabeth's neck. "She will come see me when I sleep." And in the next breath, "you hungry, Lizzie?" He was sliding off her lap, reaching for her hand and pulling her past their father to the kitchen. "I show you, here's the refrigerator with eggs and there's the toaster for bread."

She found bread for the toaster and microwave bacon. As she decided the amount to cook T.J. climbed on a tall chair to watch. Elizabeth spooned eggs onto plates as the micro wave dinged with the bacon read y and Frank came into the room. "Something smells wonderful. I haven't eaten in two days. Is there enough?" For the first time, through it all, Elizabeth smiled.

"I found your envelope. Bottom of the pile."

"Thank you." The next minutes they were all busy. "We needed that good food, Elizabeth." Troubled eyes met hers. "Will you be with us for a small celebration of Sarah's life? Tomorrow?"

"That soon?" T.J. was slipping down from the tall chair. Automatically she wiped his hands.

"It's the third day. Her body was cremated. It will be mostly office personnel, Elizabeth."

"Cremated?"

"Her request. She said her body was riddled with cancer." As always his last words were almost indistinguishable. "She planned it knowing I would be at a loss." His shoulders slumped in defeat.

"What time?"

"Ten in the morning."

"I will but then I leave to go home to Mother."

"Of course." Two words was all he said, but she heard more, "I need you, Elizabeth. Please stay."

The next day, Elizabeth drove to the Hamilton Funeral Parlor on East Main to honor Sarah's life. T.J. claimed her immediately, holding her hand so tight it hurt. She pulled him next to her body as they sit and leaned down to kiss the top of his head. His hair smelled fresh. Their father was functioning. After the celebration of Sarah, sitting alone in her car Elizabeth called her mother.

"Mom, I won't be home for a few days. There are loose ends I must tie together."

****

She followed her father's car. T.J. had a hard time deciding which car to ride in but in the end, he said, "Daddy's sad. Okay?' She had tousled his hair and told him he was doing the right thing. The one thing she had resolved not to do was happening and she seemed unable to control it. She was feeling T.J.'s affection, trying to check it off to the wiles of a child knowing all the while she could easily adore him. How absurd that she of all people was becoming concerned for his days ahead when the reality of his mother's absence set in. She heard their dad telling him to go change out of his best clothes.

"We should have had a brunch for those people," Frank said as they entered the house. "I had no idea that many would attend. In fact I thought it would be just the three of us."

"Dad, I know you have friends and she must have, there was at least a hundred people there. As quickly as it all happened that's quite a lot of people considering the obituary has not made the paper yet."

"It hasn't?"

"No." Elizabeth shrugged out of the navy jacket that matched her dress as T.J. came from his room wearing only boxer shorts with superman logo and socks and shoes. Elizabeth laughed as his hands went wide and he shrugged bony little shoulders. "You got a problem?"

"No clothes."

Following him back to his room, she asked, "Do you mean as they are all dirty or the drawer is empty?"

"They're little. Momma was sick and we don't have any."

Frank stood in the door listening. "That's probably true, they're too little and the ones that fit are in the wash. Sarah could not shop the last months. I'll take you to get clothes that fit, Buddy."

"Superman?"

Frank laughed, "well, maybe one set." His eyes met Elizabeth's. "You always wanted ice princesses."

"Why don't we go now? We can grab a bite to eat and then find the proper Superman outfit?"

"Perfect," Frank replied. "Only been here ten minutes and the house is closing in on me."

Chapter 4

Elizabeth had a lot of thinking to do as she drove home to her mother in Mosby. How could she explain the delay in coming home without mentioning her father or T.J. Of course that would be by accident if she slipped up and mentioned them. She just could not make that mistake. Her mother would be furious. To this day she felt she was not only betrayed but that anyone who mentioned Frank was her enemy. She had cut ties with most of her friends because they remembered Frank as the fun loving hard working man that he was. Most could not believe he had strayed from Nancy Ann's bed. When she overheard two women whispering at the Newspaper office it was probably her fault, Nancy Ann stopped her subscription to the Mosby Times and said she would never list and ad in that worthless rag again and if her name was bandied around town she would see they were fired.

When the Ladies Society of the First Baptist Church of Mosby called, she ignored them, until one who was president took it upon herself to make a house visit and in so doing, insulted Nancy Ann when she offered counsel on how to make your husband happy. Nancy Ann quit the church and though she was against speaking in tongues, if she wished to attend a church she went to the Pentecostal Assembly and to her delight found it wasn't mandatory one speak in tongues, it merely showed vetted fellowship if one did.

How she would treat her daughter, was another thing, entirely. There was still enough child in Elizabeth she could not suffer the silence, the terrible times of being shut out of her mother love. They suffered enough as she was growing into an adult, but that was one thing and this was another.

Nancy Ann was out the door, hurrying down the path as Elizabeth arrived. "Where have you been?" Nancy Ann was out of breath but beautiful. Her hair was coifed, nails manicured and beneath the cotton duster she was wearing, Elizabeth had a peek at her best undies, saved for special times, only.

"If you don't hurry you are going to be late."

"Late for what?" She watched her mother sit a small suitcase on the first step of the stairs and whirl around to face her.

"Oh, no, have you forgotten? This is the weekend all the group that left Mosby for College was to come home for a, what did Sybil Collier call it?" She had one hand to her mouth as if that helped. "A Soiree? Is that a gathering with lots of music and dance? Well, she was the chair person and takes all the credit...which is just as well, I stayed as long as I could help but when they sit and started gossiping I left. I figured they'd get to me or your father...by the way, do you know how he's doing and that woman. Rachael, is it or Esther... some woman's name from the Bible."

"Mother."

"Well, I think that's right. Anyway, I just knew you'd bring home a gorgeous dress and probably meet that Derek Larson person for the, whatever it's called. I think of it as a prom and it will be so much fun."

"You're going?"

"Well, I was asked to be in charge of refreshments. You know, watchdog type thing. It's in the school cafeteria and no alcoholic beverage is allowed and not one of the other women felt they were strong minded enough to reprimand whoever tries to bring it in and they knew I could, so yes, I'm going."

"That's interesting." She tilt her head studying her mother. "Do you do this type of thing often?"

"I see that gleam in your eye. You're making fun of me. I moped around her for three years and what did it get me? Nothing. All the while your father, who we both know is my age, was dilly dallying with a young woman not much older than his daughter."

"How do you know that? You never told me."

"For heaven's sakes, Elizabeth, haven't you learned anything? Women are astute. They have ways of finding the answers to their own personal problems and that woman was definitely a problem to me."

"Did you encounter her, Mother, I mean attack her? I'm finding out things I had no idea about."

Nancy Ann slid into the Queen Anne Chair at the foot of the stairs. "I'm tired just talking about her, maybe it's because its linked to your father…" She settled into the chair as her mind tried to settle, too. I thought I'd left the anger behind but something today has made it rise up full force. Surely your father won't return home for this party. Sybil said it would be similiar to a reunion, only with purpose."

"The purpose being…?"

"Honoring the ones who graduated from Mosby and are ready to graduate college." She sighed deeply. "Now, where is your dress and what about Derek?"

"I tried calling him but was unable to reach him. Don't you have a dress I can wear?"

"Elizabeth, you never took important dates so so so….lightly. We might find one of your old dresses."

"Well…hoo-hoo for us. You must have fever. You never liked Derek Larson and I haven't heard from him."

"I couldn't stand it if your dad came and brought her."

Looping her arm around her mother, Elizabeth said, "You never change. I thought we were talking about me." They started up the stairs. "You are sure this is a formal occasion."

"Yes, I was on that committee, too."

"Well, well, well. You are branching out, aren't you."

"Elizabeth, please. I'm this close to crying." Nancy Ann put her index to her thumb. "I will always be humiliated by what your dad has done I couldn't stand it if he turned up with her when I've been on so many of the committees. It just makes me a nervous wreck. Someday you will understand."

Shaking her head, Elizabeth wondered, should she tell her? Surely, it would be even more unsettling. "Let's find a dress I can still fit in," she said, instead. "This should be interesting my mother there, but then Catrin's mother always managed to be lurking in the back ground. Tell you what, if Derek doesn't show…maybe you can be my dance partner. You did say dancing, didn't you?"

****

The events of the week had made Elizabeth feel amazingly old, while being involved in life had made Nancy Ann look surprisingly ten years younger. The two giggled as they dressed for the Soiree'. "Why didn't you all just call it a ball?" Elizabeth asked.

"Sybil said that was altogether too common," Nancy Ann replied. "She's the boss, you know."

"I'll try Derek's cell once more." Elizabeth dialed but there was no reply. "Hmm. Where do you suppose he is?"

Nancy Ann was smiling. "I don't know and as you said moons ago, I don't care. I really like my grown up daughter. I have missed you so much. Do you think when you graduate you will come home more often?"

"That depends on where I find a job, don't you think? Come on, climb into my carriage."

"How do you feel in your restyled gown?"

Elizabeth laughed. "What if we'd ruined it pulling that ruffle from around the neck?"

"I think they're made that way so if a person wants to change something. No one will ever know.

That's why you wouldn't wear it for the eleventh grade prom. You hated ruffles." Nancy Ann took a deep breath. "I was wrong, instead we went out and bought one that cost more and had less style and as I remember you were in hog heaven. No ruffles, no lace, just about like what you're wearing, simple with a pearl necklace, diamond studs and wedges. If I were you I'd have a pair of those six inch heels."

"No one sees our feet and I want to be comfortable, not tormented. If my feet hurt, I hurt all over."

Pulling into the drive, they could hear the band warming up. A lot of people had arrived and were milling around outside. "Good thing the weather's mild today. It could have been snow."

"It's early." Nancy Ann pointed, "Park over by the Solarium, dear. It makes a shorter walk for us."

"My this doesn't look like our old school, a Solarium with its own Rose garden. The Schoolboard daddies must be richer than ever. Hmm? By the way, do you remember the snow man we built?"

"Don't remind me." Nancy Ann turned to place a kiss on her daughter's forehead. "I'm so glad you are home. Being alone is like a disease. You don't know what to do next. I love you."

"I love you, too, Mother." Elizabeth was scanning the building, looking for Derek. Now that she had arrived she was feeling a surge of joy, knowing he would be holding her in his arms tonight. Her heart beat a little faster. At that moment a flashy little sport car pulled into the drive. "Who is that?"

Nancy Ann stopped to look. "That would be your old friend, Catrin." She turned toward the room that housed the trophies. "Have fun, darling and I'll see you later."

Stepping behind the nearest column, out of Catrin's sight, Elizabeth watched. As usual, Catrin was smiling her brightest at the man by her side, hooking an arm inside his and never once losing step with him as they walked toward the solarium. Turning aside, she avoided reuniting with Catrin and her date. She would feel much more at ease doing that when she was on Derek's arm. But she couldn't help admiring the man's cobalt blue jacket. As true of all Catrin's dates, he wore his clothes well.

Taking one last glance at herself in the long windows of the Solarium, Elizabeth entered the building. Already couples were on the floor, dancing to the orchestra playing Moon River, appropriate for the atmosphere of the night. Outside a full moon was shining down on a hundred different people with a hundred different plans for the future. Elizabeth was unsure what the night held for her. A job had been offered since she spoke with her mother, the text coming in while she dressed saying a letter was in the mail. It was the corporations hope that she would consider their offer. The main office was in Chicago but a part of their corporation was located in a small town a hundred miles North of Mosby.

Catrin was on the dance floor, wearing the six inch heels her mother mentioned, the split of her dress going dangerously high on the thigh as she gyrated to the music with a Congo beat. For the most part, the man stood still, lending a hand and laughing as she swung her long hair seductively around his shoulders. Elizabeth shook her head, Catrin would never change. When the music stopped Catrin fell into the gentleman's arms, her body sliding provocatively down the length of his as she managed to place her hands on his shoulders and claim his lips. The kiss last as everyone surrounding the dance floor clapped enthusiastically. Possessively, she took his hand to lead him from the dance floor. For some unknown reason, the man glanced to where Elizabeth was standing, stopping suddenly with his feet braced blocking further movement as Catrin was forced to find where his gaze was going.

Elizabeth gasped. Catrin was asking what he saw, no doubt, because he pointed toward her. Catrin could not see her behind the column but Derek could until she moved and then Elizabeth did what her mind said to do. She ran. Ducking behind a giant Boxwood, she removed the wedges, grabbed handfuls of skirt and ran the whole length of the Solarium garden, fell into her car and sped out of the parking lot. A mile down the road she slipped into a second drive to a private residence and hurriedly sent a text to her mother. "I saw something I wish I hadn't. I'm sick at my stomach. If you see Derek do not tell him I'm home. Repeat. You have not seen me and probably won't. As far as he is concerned I'm not here."

Nancy Ann text back. "I have to stay after the Soirre' ends. Marg can bring me home. Get some rest."

Elizabeth was too tired to cry. For awhile she leaned across the steering wheel trying to get her bearings. So Derek and Catrin did get together while they were away at the same school. That pretty much cinched the job offer. She had to live somewhere. A hundred miles away wasn't that far if her mother needed her. She drove on home, changed into pajamas and let her hair down. She heard wheels crunch on the gravel drive and went to the window. From behind the drapes she saw Derek run to the front porch and then heard the frantic beating on the door.

"Lizzie, let me in. I know you're in there. Talk to me, Lizzie. Talk to me." He sounded as if he was crying. So was she. "Lizzie, it's not what you think. Lizzie."

It was midnight when her mother came home. She sat on the edge of the sofa, placing one hand on Elizabeth. "Do you want to talk about it?"

"Not yet."

"I'm here, when you do." She was back shortly, in her own pajamas, taking Elizabeth by the hand to lead her to the bedroom she used to share with Frank. The covers were turned back. She motioned for Elizabeth to get into bed and then crawled in beside her and pulled her daughter into her arms. "Sometimes," she said in a soft voice, "things hurt us so deeply we can't talk about them until years later and that's okay."

The next morning Nancy Ann awakened to find Elizabeth still in her bed, staring at her as if she had something to say. "Yes? I know that look, it never changes, not from when you were a little girl or now. I suspect when you marry you will still have that look on your face when you want to say something."

Elizabeth was still weighing the pros and cons of what she was about to tell her mother.

"You are struggling. What are you going to say; that you are leaving before noon and please don't cry?" Tears stung Nancy Ann's eyes. "Well, I will cry because I'm so tired of being alone, Elizabeth."

Her daughter kept staring, not a blink or movement of the body, just staring. "Okay, what is it? Life is hard. You have no idea how hard it is, Elizabeth." Nancy reached up to pull her hair out from under her shoulder. "Could you trim my hair while you're here? I don't like going to the shop and if I do she always cuts one side longer than the other. You're nodding. You will? Okay. Thank you, darling. Now, back to being alone. I hate it. I've thought of renting a gardener, since I don't have a pool and can't rent a pool boy. Or, maybe a tutor, what do you think about that, he could teach me a new language."

"I think you're crazy." Elizabeth pulled the cover over Nancy's head. "Where would you go that you need a new language?" She leaned up on one elbow staring down into her mother's face. "Are you really lonely, Mother?"

Tears rimmed Nancy's eyes, ready to overflow. "Yes, I know I should have adjusted but I thought there would be someone, not just anyone but your father to grow old with. I get it, he quit loving me. I don't even know what I did wrong." The tears rolled down her cheeks and she used the sheet to wipe them away. After a sniffle or two, she said, "this is supposed to be about you. What's going on?"

A war was going on in Elizabeth's head, whether to tell her mother what she saw, whether to tell her about Sarah dying and the little two year old boy whose clothes were too little and his daddy who seemed at loose ends and didn't know where to turn and that she was afraid he wouldn't take care of himself and would die earlier than the doctor said he might. It was only yesterday when her mother was afraid he would embarrass her further in the nosey little town of Mosby. Since last night she was experiencing a few moods herself, wondering that Derek betrayed her right there on the dance floor. But then she hadn't been in touch with him the last week, he was probably getting even with her.

Didn't men do that sort of thing? How would she know, her father left his whole family for another woman,? At least she and Derek were not married. She decided her personal problem came in second to T.J. and her fathers. Still, she wasn't sure the time was right to unload the whole sad mess on her mother.

"You are scaring me. It took you forever to tell us when you nearly burned down the little house out back where we had my mother's china and silverware stored and a very expensive violin. When you finally told us all that was damaged was one china plate. We thought the violin was gone for good but it was up high and the flames hadn't reached that far. Well, we learned a lesson. That violin came inside."

Leaning on her elbow, again peering down into Nancy's face, Elizabeth began, "Mom, you may want to kill me, or you might ask me to leave. I haven't betrayed you, Mother. It's just that life has these little curves and sometimes I'm not good at making them."

Nancy Ann groaned, once more covering her face with the covers. "I knew it. It's bad. Are you pregnant?"

Indignant, Elizabeth slapped her mother's hand. "I don't even have a boyfriend. That is a requirement isn't it? I mean the other gender? No, I'm saving myself." She pulled the cover away.

"I'm dying here, Elizabeth. Just tell me."

"Do I need to get the straight jacket? Or, do you promise to lay real still and listen until I'm finished?"

Reluctantly, Nancy Ann nodded and did the sign of zipping her lips.

"Not good enough. To the finish?"

A deep sigh came from Nancy Ann. "I will." Elizabeth appeared dubious. "I will. I promise."

"Close your eyes and just listen." Elizabeth watched her mother close her eyes. Elizabeth began. "As you know, I told you I had loose ends to clear up. Well, that was kind of true. Two days before break, early in the morning I was in deep sleep when I received a call. I'll tell you later about the caller. Would I come to the hospital, family was dying? Reluctantly, I went. The next question was, "Would you care for my child, please?" I know nothing about a child but I felt sorry for the person. Yes, I will. "Please, take my child to this address. I did that, too. When the parent came home, I started to leave and was ask, "would you please stay?" I was supposed to come home to you but the death had left a very unsettled loved one that seemed unable to function normally, I suppose death has that effect on us. I stayed another day. The little person had outgrown his clothes and was in need. I accompanied the parent shopping, prepared a meal and comforted the little one by use of a rocking chair, all the while feeling very inadequate as I wondered how I had gotten in that predicament. Long story short, the parent that remains is in very bad health and needs help, not just paid help, but human kindness to keep on going help and it concerns me and I don't know what to do, whether to become involved."

They both took a deep breath and stared hard at each other as Elizabeth sit up, pummeled the pillow and placed it against the headboard to scoot against. Nancy Ann did the same. For a bit they sat there, heads tilted, rethinking the dilemma that wasn't their's and yet they knew about it.

"I'm almost afraid to reply. This could be your father, except the grapevine says the girl lost the baby."

"What girl?"

"I thought you knew. That's why it hurt so deeply. Your father got a girl, not much older than you, pregnant, but Sybil who keeps tracks of everything says she lost the baby. Miscarriage."

"What did Dad tell you?"

"That there was some kind of problem, a friend of his secretary died, he only meant to comfort her and ended up taking her home and sleeping with her."

"I see." Disgusted with her father she asked, "was that out of consideration or availability?

"Well," indignation was in Nancy's voice. "I didn't and I don't. George, the mailman's wife died but when I said I'm sorry to hear that, George, I did not invite him in and make love. You don't get it." Nancy started to flounce out of bed but Elizabeth laid a hand on her.

"uh, uh, uh, uh…. I get it. Someone took advantage of another, which one, I don't know, probably Dad. But you promised, to hear my story to the end. Now, forget George and tell me what do you think?"

"What do I think?" Nancy replied in a mesmerizing voice. "I think I have to be careful. You were around your lawyer father too long, you could trick me into something I can't handle and it doesn't take much. Why don't we cut to the chase and you," her voice raised a pitch, "tell me what I need to know."

"Do you remember the girl's name?"

"What girl?" Nancy was feeling a surge of resentment in remembering that was morphing into anxiety. "You mean your Daddy's intended?" She meant for it to sound sarcastic and it did. "No, I don't have that information…my saved photo is your dad breaking his vows. That was enough."

"Her name was Sarah," Elizabeth said softly. "Sarah."

"You met her?"

"Not really, but kinda, sorta." She saw her mother's hurt expression. "It wasn't a happy occasion."

"Tell me."

"She was dying."

"She's dead?" Nancy's face dissolved into confusion, sadness, frustration. "I'm not a bad person, Lizzie. I never would wish that on my worst enemy…I don't think I would, anyway. How did she die?"

"Cancer."

"And you know this because…."

"I'm the person Dad called to come to the hospital to take care of the little boy."

"There's a child? Wow. I mean that kind of knocks the breath out of me. I haven't seen your father in three years and to think his life went on while mine stood still. I mean, I have to adjust to this…."

"I understand. I had to grab the reality of what I was experiencing, quickly. I mean it took some doing."

"Forget the child. You said your father was at loose ends. You mean he isn't coping well?"

"No, he isn't and I don't know what he will do, since he has health issues of his own and a child needs daily attention, doesn't it?"

Nancy Ann's shoulders drooped. "I guess that means you are leaving me, going back to help him."

"You can come with me, but you have to stay at my apartment. It's out of the question for you to go There with out me. I can't have you…well, you know. You and I can't fight over this circumstance."

****

"It's time to go. Try to rest while I'm gone." Elizabeth studied her mother. "You are so restless, I can't take you with me, you would hop out of the car and come bounding up the steps and not only would Dad be shocked, the little boy would be completely confused."

"Did I ask to go with you?" Nancy plopped down into the nearest chair. "No, I did not." She sighed.

"It would be humiliating, to say the least."

Her mother seemed to have shrunk. Was she always that small? Elizabeth paused for a moment, Thinking, if she was the mother what would she want? "For heaven's sakes," she said. "Come on, but I need to think, promise you won't rattle all the way? And you will have to stay at my apartment."

"Rattle?" Nancy Ann hurried into the bedroom and came back with an already packed overnighter. "I thought you might want company if you had to return to check on your father, and Elizabeth, for all the sarcasm you hear coming out of this mouth, I do still have Christian concerns about your father. You have no idea what I've gone through here, with the nosey questions, people's unsolicited advice and the church people thinking everything my fault. I've had wide shoulders, in order to exist and I didn't tell you." They rode the miles, mostly in a comfortable silence, and when they reached College City she left Nancy Ann at her apartment. "If you need me, here's the number but don't do anything foolish. No taxi's to Dad's house. It might upset him."

"Lord knows we don't want to upset your Dad," Nancy murmured. "That's my department."

She relived the conversation as she pulled into her father's drive. "Please be home," she whispered as she rang the doorbell. She didn't hear a sound coming from the house and finally turned to leave, when the door opened and Frank, wearing an apron pushed it even wider for her to enter.

"Elizabeth." He pecked a kiss on her cheek. "Come into the kitchen. We are trying to fry chicken legs and make cookies."

"At the same time?" She entered the kitchen to the onslaught of T.J.'s nearly knocking her off her feet as he ran to hug her. "Umm," she caught her breath, bringing T.J. up for a hug. "That's pretty amazing." She surveyed the scene. Flour all over the counter, a bottle of oil and at least eight chicken legs ready for the pan which was practically smoking on the stove. "Let's lower the flame and let the oil cool before we drop these pieces in."

"Now, the oven is on four hundred and I'm pretty sure the box for the cookies probably said three fifty." Her Dad dug the box out of the trash to confirm or deny.

"You're right," he replied. "We haven't been in here very long and I am worn out." She was studying him as he passed an arm across his face. "I know. I know. Everything's a mess and I don't know what to do."

She patted his back. "You're doing fine, but sit down and let me see if I can get things in control."

"Why are you here?" He grinned. "Not that you aren't needed and always welcome, but why?"

"To check on you and T.J. and see how things are going."

"I guess you're seeing, huh?" He grinned seeing T.J. pressing a cookie block flat.

She smiled in return as she asked, "When's your next doctor appointment?"

"Let me see, it should be right here on this calendar, let's see the date for my appointment is," He glanced her way, in shock. "It's actually this afternoon. This afternoon? How can I make that? Barely two hours from now and I'm standing in a kitchen covered in flour." Opening the oven door he slid in a tray with chopped blocks of cookie dough. "I can't take T.J.; there are rules."

"You don't have to. I'm here and we can hold down the fort, right T.J.?"

****

"I'll be longer than intended," she told her Mother over the phone. "Dad has a doctor appointment."

"How does he look?"

"Pretty haggard. His color is off, leaning toward gray."

"Hmmm. Put her picture away."

"I can't. It hangs in T.J.'s room. It's his comfort marker. Love you, Mom, gotta go." T.J. was waiting.

"Come on, Boyo, let's see if we can put these puzzles together. Are they always left in here?"

"Yes, so me and Momma can find them and she doesn't have to get out of her chair." Suddenly his eyes filled with tears and he pushed his head against her thinking she couldn't see them.

"It's all right to cry, T.J. Your Momma loved you and you loved her. We cry when we miss people we love." She picked him up, for a moment, holding him close and then sit him back down. "Bet I can beat you putting the puzzle together."

He was amazingly fast for a two year old and beat her. When the door bell rang she cautioned him not to open it. "We don't know who it is and we have to be careful who we let into the house. Okay?"

T.J. backed up to the sofa, his eyes solemn as he replied, "Okay."

Elizabeth opened the door, shock registering on her face. "Mother?"

Nancy Ann pushed past her. "I decided to see for myself, how the Daddy looks." Her eyes were on T.J. "So, who are you?" She sit on the edge of the sofa, studying the somber look on his face.

T.J. was looking at Nancy and then Elizabeth. "Do we know her?"

Elizabeth smiled. "I know her. She is my mother. T.J. meet my mother, Nancy Ann Turner."

"We have the same last name."

"Yes, we do," Nancy replied, extending her hand. "That's not so bad, is it?"

"I don't know." He put his hand in hers, looking to Elizabeth. "Is it? Okay?"

Trying to hide her own confusement why her mother was there she said, "Yes, I believe it's just fine."

"Do you want to put puzzles together?" He asked.

"I can try," Nancy agreed, slipping off the sofa into the floor.

"What do I call you?"

"How about Nancy?"

"I have a book the boy calls his grandmother Nan. Can I call you Nan?"

Nancy's eyes cut to Elizabeth. "I think that will work, what do you think, Elizabeth?"

"I'm sure it will," Elizabeth said in a sing song voice. "I'm still trying to figure out why you're here."

"I came to smell the roses. You seem to be having all the fun. I always wanted to know what a little boy was like compared to a little girl."

"You worry me."

"I am harmless. I didn't even bring a purse. It's a good thing I had a twenty in my pocket." Before long, T.J. was showing signs of needing a nap and crawled into his bed when Elizabeth told him he must. She padded back into the living room finding her mother restacking the puzzles.

"He said they go on the shelf under the table so his mother could find them easily."

"Mother? The two stared at each other. "I must say, Mother, I'm trying to figure out the reason you're here."

"I can leave if it bothers you."

"Just tell me why and maybe I can deal with it."

"You are too serious. I've never been bound to territory, is that what you expect? Me to back off, let you and your dad become family again and I have to listen to your being together, or maybe you would keep me out in the cold and never mention one word about the little boy who is your brother."

"Frankly, I hadn't decided, other than the fact I don't want to see him hurt."

Nancy's hands went up. "Who'se hurting anyone? Not me. I was just curious."

"What if Dad doesn't want you here?"

Nancy huffed. "Right now, he doesn't know what he wants and if it is as you say....

He'll get over it. I'm deciding my options, you might say planning my skirmish."

"Skirmish?" For the first time, Elizabeth began to wonder if her mother was mentally sound. "I don't understand, though skirmish fits you perfectly, but then there's a little boy to consider. Right?"

"Don't give me that look. I know you. Remember? I'm not crazy nor vindictive where a child is concerned but your father, I might enjoy leading him around by a hook in the nose for a while."

"Ouch." Elizabeth closed her eyes as she shook her head. "That's what I'm afraid of. I don't know How you got here but why don't you go back to the apartment and I'll be there shortly."

The door opened and Frank stepped inside. "Nancy?" The surprise on his face was evident second to the painful expression he wore when he first opened the door. He was doing his best to recover. "I didn't expect to see you."

"No, I don't imagine you did," her voice was brusque.

"Did you come to gloat?"

"Actually, I followed our daughter and landed here. I've met your son and we've mastered the puzzles together. I didn't know you had a son."

"Yeah, well I do. A boy without a mother. That should be something for you to swallow."

"You look terrible. Still living life according to your rules?"

"You haven't changed."

"From what I'm seeing you haven't either. Maybe in becoming the child's sole parent you'll find time to take care of yourself."

"That is long past your business," he replied, wearily passing a hand over his eyes as though he did not know which way to turn or where to go from there. His eyes rest on Elizabeth, almost pleading.

"All right, you two. You're a bit old to be bickering like this." She picked up her jacket. "Dad, T.J. is sound asleep and we will be going. I'll see you in the next day or so."

"I guess your mother will be heading home."

"I'm right here, Frank, not quite as invisible as you always thought. I actually speak up now."

"Perhaps you shouldn't." He sank into the recliner, allowing the foot rest to pop forward and elevate his feet on a level with his body. "Forgive me, I'm tired."

"What did the doctor say?"

Frank didn't look at Elizabeth. "He said I'm going to live. For now."

She stopped to kiss his forehead. "Try to rest, Dad, and call if you need me." She detoured to the kitchen to pick up her purse.

Nancy couldn't resist, she bent over the chair arm and placed a kiss on Frank's cheek. "Poor Baby now you'll know how I felt when you left me."

"You're wrong, Nancy, nothing here compares. Someone died."

"No, Frank, you're wrong. I grieved because in my world, you left me alone. It's the same. You died."

Elizabeth returned to see her father pointing to the door with a look of anger in his eyes and her mother laughing as she went out.

"Mother." She was shaking her head. "What did you do, or what did you say to him?"

"Am I bad?" Nancy Ann's laughter bore a hysterical note, "I told him now he'd know how I felt when I was left alone."

"And?"

"He said there was a difference, someone died. I disagreed. It's the same. Grieving is grieving."

"Get in the car."

"I can walk if you prefer."

"Five miles? I don't think so." Elizabeth waited for her mother to climb in. "Now, buckle up. You're acting like a child."

"You're the expert." Nancy Ann's sarcasm wasn't lost on her daughter.

"I don't like you tonight."

"That's fine. I don't like you either." Nancy Ann turned to lay her head where she could look out the window and was almost immediately asleep. The drama and anxiety had worn her to the bone.

****

"You aren't going back to Mosby?" Nancy asked as Elizabeth parked outside her apartment and got out.

"Now what makes you think that?"

Nancy was clearly irritated with her child. "You can cut the sarcasm. I'll go home tomorrow if you aren't going back. But I thought you had decided to spend your days with me at Safe Haven."

"I may have a new plan, one that includes helping care for T.J." She hung her jacket in the closet. "A child is deserving of a family caring for him, isn't he? Dad can't do it alone, especially sick."

Nancy Ann collected her overnight case, made sure the keys were in her purse and with sad eyes, said "Good bye, Elizabeth. If you ever need me or just want to visit. You know where to find me."

****

The next week was miserable for Nancy Ann. She doubt Elizabeth would give a second thought to her being left alone again while Elizabeth was busy helping with T.J. It wasn't that she was jealous, there seemed to be a double standard. She did take Frank's illness into consideration but Frank always got his way. She was invited to come for Thanksgiving dinner but turned down the offer. A drive there and back in frigid weather wasn't tempting and she couldn't stomach the acidity of their relationship. The day after, spending time with Marge and Margie, who were both alone, she was in the basement sorting through boxes of Christmas garlands, ornaments and a number of ceramic snowmen when the phone rang.

"Nancy Ann?" No one said her name like he did.

"Frank."

"I sense a time of trouble between you and our daughter."

"Really? Then you must be physic."

"No, no, no," he cut her off. "What happened to her boyfriend? Did your run him off?"

"I beg your pardon. I haven't really talked with Derek Larson in years but he was at the last Mosby social with Catrin Collier on his arm. I thought they were meeting up, but guess I was wrong."

"How did he turn out?"

"I don't know. Why?"

"There was a time I felt you didn't think he was good enough for our daughter."

"It wasn't that, I didn't want any mistakes to happen to prevent her getting a degree."

"Well, two more months and she will have that. But first Christmas. T. J. is excited. How about you?"

"The last few years the holidays have been depressing."

"That's hard to believe of you, you always loved decorating the house, the yard and every thing else."

She took a deep breath and decided to let him talk. When he was tired enough he'd hang up."

"Nancy Ann?" There was a long pause. "Could I bring T.J. to Safe Haven for Christmas?"

She took a deep breath. "This surprises me. Why?"

"It's always been one of my favorite places and I'd like for T.J. to have a run through the meadow behind the house, maybe climb one of those big old oaks and I guess the tree house is still there at the end of the property that Elizabeth and Derek built, isn't it?"

She didn't know if the tree house was still stable. "What did you have in mind, Frank?"

"Christmas is on Monday and we close the office Friday morning so everyone can have time to shop."

"I'm listening." What was he thinking if it was cold and what if it snowed, T. J. in the meadow?

"Could we drive in early Friday evening? I'll help you with whatever it takes to care for all of us. I know Elizabeth will want to be there. She and T.J. have become close…"

'I see."

"If you already have plans, I understand."

"No, it's fine. We can do what you want but there's supposed to be a winter storm coming in.

Relief sound in his voice when he said, "Thank you, Nan. We will see you Friday the twenty second." Then he was laughing. "Snow? That will be even more fun, won't it Nan? See you then."

"Nan?" She hung up the phone. Nan was the word between her and T.J. Go figure.

****

Two hours later, Marg called. "What's your thoughts?" She asked, telling about the call.

"You say Frank has cancer and a little boy too, but you don't know how serious? I think Frank feels badly how he's treated you and wants to spend a few hours making amends for years of pain. The Rat."

"Just before the call I had talked myself out of decorating. Now I'm in to it again."

Marg groaned. With a roll of her eyes, she said, "that lets me out. I can't afford to fall off the Ladder."

"How about you come over anyway and stand on the floor and hand things to me?" Nancy was smiling.

****

"IT's beginning to look a lot like Christmas." Nancy checked the garland wrapped around the four white columns of the front porch, hung the large wreath, adjusted the red ribbon and did a little dance on the coco-mat in front of the door that lit up when you stepped on it. It played a little song to boot. "In my front yard." She felt such a happy glow seeing the tree sparkling inside the window. How could she really have heavy burdens to bear? But she did. Elizabeth hadn't called and except for Frank telling her their daughter was now working in his office, she would not have known. Was she so wrong to have gone to Frank's house right after the little boy's mother died? Evidently, because Elizabeth had not spoken to her since. It hurt but there was nothing she could do about it.

Now, they were coming to Safe Haven for four days. She wondered how Elizabeth felt about that.

She suspected Elizabeth's aloofness had more to do with something else happening than just what she had done. Probably, Derek Larson was in the mix. She hadn't thought he would be Catrin's type but then he had become quite popular due to his athletic skills. Still, Catrin never stayed with any one long. It wasn't that she thought her daughter too good for Derek, she was aware of his family history and there was always a myth that what happened in a family did form the child and his parents had both abandoned him. But his grandfather was a good man and had seen to the boy being raised right.

Three days before guest arrived, Nancy was priding herself on not falling off the ladder or down the basement steps when in the kitchen, something caught beneath her feet and she went flying across the room, found her foot hung in the kitchen table and twist her ankle. The pain was so intense she called Marg and ask her to take her to the doctor.

"I can't believe you did all the heavy decorating and then twist your ankle." She drove Nancy to the doctor and picked up the pain prescription from the pharmacy. "He said stay off that foot, friend. I think that is good advice if you want to be up and around when your guest arrive." She studied Nancy. "I don't know why but I think you are looking forward to Christmas, for a change, and I'm glad."

Chapter 5

Eighteen Years Later

Snow began falling as Elizabeth left Chicago. There were traveler warnings but traffic kept the roads operable to St. Louis. Six hours at the wheel was enough for the first day. She could finish the trip to Mosby the next and whether gripping the wheel or the stress she'd encountered with Addison before leaving she was tired. With a hot shower and food from the hotel menu she fell into bed planning to leave the hotel by ten the next morning. For the most part, it was smooth driving from St. Louis on, but an occasional vehicle sitting on the roadside was enough to keep her cautious. Nearing her destination the secondary roads became more hazardous as snow was falling near blizzard condition; what should have taken two hours driving became four. Reaching Mosby she found the streets were already deep ruts as she put the jeep in four wheel drive and searched for sign or land marks she hadn't seen in five years. Trees had grown and new buildings had sprung up but then she saw the Park. Now, if she could find the street marker in this secluded place. No doubt it would be covered in snow and hard to see.

Elizabeth saw the sign, practically hidden in an overgrown bush. Safe Haven. How many times had people come to the door asking if Safe Haven was a lodge. "No," her mother often replied. "This was my mother's family home, passed down through the generations and someone in the family named it. There have been many signs replaced, but the house still stands, one hundred and twenty year old."

She turned where the road forked, one heading toward the house, the other led down to where the tree stand was and the grove of trees the uncles had put in, a choice spot for turkey hunting.

She was as surprised as anyone when her mother called from Florida asking her to check on the house. That conversation had been almost two months past and sparked consideration to move back.

"Is it okay, Mother, if I stay a day or two?"

"Darling, I won't be coming back to Safe Haven. If you want to sell it, just send me half of whatever you get for it, otherwise enjoy your stay at the house. I have decided Florida is a good place to live."

"Want to tell me why you really are interested in Florida?" She heard her mother's laughter. "I think you've found someone and one day you will tell me. Right?" Of course her mother did not reply.

She pulled into the drive that Jeremy Johnson had carved out of the lawn, a half circle access to the house, whereas before navigating the thick grass of the lawn was a chore. "Honey, we never thought about changing anything about this big old house. Built from cedar, it's stood against the ravage of weather and time," Nancy Ann was prone to say in her lilting southern accent. "It was Grandmother's home and we always came here when she called to us. Then Mother and Daddy moved here and in time it fell to me. All I've done was keep up that which wears out…cedar's pretty trusty."

Now, Elizabeth surmised, it was becoming hers. She didn't know when she actually decided to return to Mosby. Married to Addison Kinder had advantages. She moved easily about in the big city circles but compared to her father's discretion, Addison made Frank Turner look like a choir boy. She had many ghosts from the past to face but more recently stand up realities had slapped her in the face. She didn't want to deal with them, she simply wanted out. The first three years were tolerable, but the last five were pure hell. Addison became sloppy and surly and defiant when faced with his transgressions.

He mocked her stupidity concerning his latest fling. "My dear, we've been at this for ages."

"It doesn't matter," she said. "She can have you. I'm leaving."

"But where will you go?" She ignored him. Later, he wouldn't remember anyway."

"Another man won't want you, Sweetheart. You are used goods. You don't have a job. You can't survive. I won't fund you, I don't care what the divorce lawyer says, I wash my hands of you."

"You are so wrong," She replied. "Back in Mosby no one cares. They don't pass judgement. And they help those who can't help themselves and after you…it will be a very long time til I look at a man."

"You will be calling me when the bills come due."

"Are you forgetting my salary has always been equal if not more than yours?"

He gave a ridiculous laugh, "But there are no jobs in little ole Mosby for someone like you. What will you do, work as a house maid?"

"If you weren't so drunk, I'd think you were crazy, but you are and I've wasted all these years on you."

"Good luck in that mausoleum you call Safe Haven. Even your mother left little ole Mosby."

****

Not knowing what she would find, it was no surprise to see the windows covered in plywood. Why? Why had her mother boarded up the windows and who had ripped the plywood from the doors? Then it hit her; Nancy Ann Turner had not planned to return, but what was the last straw that would make her leave Safe Haven forever? She had always loved her ancestral home.

She pulled around to the back. A fallen tree blocked entrance to the garage. She reached for the knee high boots she had placed in the back seat. Once she had them on, she tried to open the door which was not an easy feat with the snow pushing against it. Finally, she crawled out the window, glad she had placed her suitcases in the back seat because a few items she wanted to keep were in the trunk. Leaving the beautiful furniture and all the accessories she had collected for their new home had caused a moment of bitterness, but if she was to start fresh she didn't need such blatant reminders of her life with Addison.

Hopefully the call to Jeremy last week meant there would be electricity, a stack of wood in case it went out and a house that didn't smell of moth balls. She trudged through the snow to the back door, fumbled through her purse for the key ring she'd kept all these years and placed the key in the lock. Stepping inside was the biggest surprise of all, warmth permeated the room, even here in the utility room where she sit down the suitcase and walked on into the hall that led to the kitchen, then dining room and on to the living room hall accessing the bathroom and the bedrooms. Warmth. She was eternally grateful not having to skirmish for wood and work with the fireplace that was always cranky. She flipped the switch that turned off the outside lights.

A thousand memories flooded her mind; the year the tree fell over and they'd rushed to keep its branches from catching on fire as it lay on the fireplace with a real fire going inside. It was a flashback of happier times, her parents together; the figurine still sitting on the table that her father had given Nancy that played YOU LIGHT UP MY Life. The flashback continued as she glanced around the room the last year they'd all celebrated together, a completely different

Christmas the first time T.J. came to be with them and her mother had handled it like a pro. That was the time she said, "I'm tired of tripping on those initials, T.J., how do you like the name Tommy? You changed my name, I'm changing yours. What do you say?" T.J. had rushed to embrace Nancy. "Okay, Nan" he said and from that moment on he was Thomas or Tommy. "Yep, you look like a Thomas James to me, just like your Momma thought. You were Sarah's boy but I think there's room in our lives for you to be Nan's boy, too. Is that all right with you?" T.J. had smiled and said "yes mam." Even now, Elizabeth wondered at the relationship between the two. If her mother knew he would be joining her for Christmas this year, she had no doubts Nancy would be there.

She took a deep breath, if wishes come true then horses could fly. One could dream the impossible, couldn't they? She carried her suitcase into the room her parents had shared until she was in seventh grade. That was when Sarah came into his life. His secretary died and he needed a replacement. The agency sent Sarah with the background of having been raised in an orphanage, trained to excel in what Frank Turner's law practice needed, and more it seemed. The beautiful marriage her parents had known flew out the window and Sarah flew in. She would never forget the day Mosby Seniors were bussed into the city and Catrin saw Frank Turner with a woman and her son. Sadly, no one knew when the boy died. She hadn't seen her father during that time, and if the grapevine gossip knew no one told her or her mother. Now they knew that child was not Frank's but T.J. was.

Melancholy she changed into pajamas and crawled into the big old four poster bed. The weather had made the trip down to Mosby difficult but she was here now and could relax. Except she couldn't. She wandered into the kitchen, opened the frig door and was pleasantly surprised. Milk, juice, a plastic container of lunch meat and cheese and a loaf of bread met her eyes. Jeremy? No, no, men didn't think of such things. Then she had to laugh. Margie was the only other person with a key to Safe Haven. She glanced at her watch. Just because she felt it was late, it wasn't. She tried calling Margie to thank her.

Margie's voice came over the cell. "If you need me, keep calling, I'm bound to pick up. If you don't, I'll call you tomorrow and if this is our Lizzie, I'm glad you are home safe, girlie. See you tomorrow. Love Ya."

She saw the headlights as a vehicle made the half circle, backing up to head toward town. So people still checked out Safe Haven. It was always true, someone curious made the drive down the lane, then had to back to the road. It was impressive with the lights on but she had turned them off. She sat on the cane bottomed stool at the waist high bar, a counter full of open shelves beneath where her mother displayed a huge collection of copper bottom pots and pans. For a moment she thought of the collection she'd left behind with Addison. It was hard to swallow. The fact she could afford nice things had been a balm to her otherwise tormented soul, but things did not make a person happy. One minute she wanted to laugh, the next cry. Her nerves must be shot! Leaning in she examined the pans and there it was, the one she and Derek Larson nearly burn up. Why would her mother keep that one? Now her mind was on Derek. She wondered how his business prospered and if he married. Opening her cell, she typed in his name and address and read the few lines describing him. She supposed it was inevitable, one day if he returned to Mosby they would run in to each other.

****

Early the next morning she called Margie.

"I knew that would be you," Margie's voice boomed over the phone. "Are you snowed in, Honey?"

"What do you think." Elizabeth was beaming. "Can you feel this smile on my face? It is so good to hear your voice."

"I can't wait to see you, Sugar, but right now nothin's movin' in Mosby. Even the street light's on the blink. Anything you need? I can find some ole long legged boy to run it up to you if he's got a four wheeler. I'm not sure even a four wheel drive vehicle can overcome this landscape."

"I'll be eating your food while I find my way around here."

"That's good, Babe. Look in the cabinet, there's a few cans of chili, a box of cereal and all the pancake mix you care to use." Margie's laughter lit up the room where Elizabeth was standing. "Look for the soup."

"Your soup?" She opened the frig door again. "I didn't see it or I would've had it last night."

"It's frozen, Lizzie. Look in the ice compartment. I didn't want it to spoil if you decided not to come back. Oh, Sugar, someone's knocking on my door. I'll see you as soon as I can. Love you."

****

There was nothing she wanted to do after she put away her clothes. Wading through the snow to the Jeep and dragging everything in had been a chore, but she would go crazy if she had a week of being locked in due to the roads closed and snow plows hard pressed to keep up with the town's main fare.

"Who was at your door?" She asked the next day when Margie called to check on her again.

"My grandson. Wait til you see him. It's Georgie all grown up coming to check on his Gramma."

"Oh, Margie, your laughter is balm to the soul. I haven't heard much of that the last year or two."

"That bad, huh? I figured." They were both quiet a minute. "You think you'll stay or you just checkin' on the house?"

"I'll have to get a job, Margie. I might make it through one year but Addison tried to move my account, and would have except one of my friends is Vice President at the bank. He got one account but he didn't know about the other."

"The Jerk. What's your plan? You want to start a new practice in Mosby?"

"No, I'm sick of other people's problems. Presently, I'm kind of in a poor poor me syndrome and I might decide to tell a client my story and I doubt that would gain confidence. I'm pretty good in the accounting department, I kind of like the idea of trying something else for a while...I doubt anyone in this town knows I have a law degree and I hope to keep it that way. Mother said she never talked it. I guess after what happened to her and Dad had something to do with it. When did you last see her?"

"Probably about the time you did. She's been gone since...let's see July, year before last."

"Yeah, it's unnatural for us to let time add up like that, but we had so much hurt between us..."

"Where's your brother?"

"Moving on in life, Margie, come January he will begin his fourth year in college, then there's Medical

School." Pride sound in her voice. "He's a brain you know with all those grants and scholarships offered. He's the youngest in his class. Secretly, I know he and mother are staying in touch."

"That part of life was a surprise, wasn't it? You all handled it better than I could ever imagine."

"We had to work it out. Mother was the biggest surprise of all. I would never have thought it."

"Pride comes before the fall, Honey. When your daddy left and you were away at school, your mother suffered. She thought they'd grow old together and then Boom, he leaves her for a younger woman. She was destroyed. I saw her literally wither and thought she was going to die."

"So what do you think was the catalyst that brought her and T.J. together?"

"Her explanation to me, and mind you she was crying her eyes out when she told me. She said I saw a little boy whose life had been turned upside down, I felt his sadness and when he called me Nan I knew God had put us together. It didn't matter about the rest. They didn't seem to know I'd fell to the bottom of the barrel but for all Tommy's intelligence at that young age I knew and when he put his arms around my neck I decided I'd brave heaven and hell for that little fellow." Margie laughed. "You know that's when she changed his name. He was Sarah's T.J. but he became Nan's Tommy."

"Did she do that for me, Margie? Did she make my life easier as she tried to do for him?"

"Yes, she did but you didn't realize it. She act like her world was okay, so yours would be. Your daddy that loved you was gone; he was ashamed to come home to see you after that big fracas in the city and she was determined you wouldn't suffer if she could help it. She became all things a kid needs, your chauffeur, your encourager. You name it. When you left she nearly died of loneliness."

Elizabeth grew silent. "I better go, Margie," she said, finally. "I'm sure you're busy."

*****

Unused to the stretch of hours alone and little to do, she pulled on the knee boots and made her way past the Jeep to the small shop where her father kept tools for maintenance, although her mother was the one who used them. She remembered his frustration when his wife could fix about anything because her father had been a carpenter and had taught her; while his parents were college professors that relied on someone else. Once when she teased him to stick to a broom and a shovel he had pout for three days. It was the shovel Elizabeth needed. Lifting a flat stone from the concrete she found the key in its plastic pouch and unlocked the door. The shovel was where it had been for years.

She was bundled up to the point she could hardly move but managed to shovel a path to the mailbox. She wondered what was the chance of getting the Jeep from the back to the road that ran in front of the mailbox? If that was possible she could venture a drive and check out any business that might need a bookkeeper or secretary. She could not take the empty hours and she knew how to meet people.

If the tree had not blocked the path, there was a concrete drive under all the snow. True it was invisible but she had an idea where it was. Did she dare try pushing the tree? She examined the front grill of the Jeep, was it high enough not to touch? Returning to the house she found the keys and five minutes later started the Jeep, moving forward, slowly, listening for contact, getting out to be sure she could ease forward.

Holding her breath she again put the Jeep in motion. Much to her amazement, although it was her plan, the tree began to slide on the snow. It was on the concrete drive. She turned the wheel just so and the tree went to one side. Elated, she shut off the motor, made her way back to the house to change clothes amused at the feeling that had lift her spirits and made her think the world a better place.

"You are such a child," she said to the image in the visor mirror. "You have been alone too long."

******

The streets were more like an obstacle course without obstacle, the deep ruts all curves and angles where vehicles had careened into them, wheels sliding and the weight of the trucks wiping out sections of frozen crust. The Jeep climbed, sank and rolled forward according to her foot on the gas pedal. She was relieved when she saw Mueller's bookkeeping. Parking the Jeep she climbed out and went in.

"May I help you?" The red head behind the desk was scrutinizing her clothing. "You're not from around here, are you?"

"How can you tell?"

"I saw that skirt and boots in a magazine. "Did you buy all three pieces? I can't see your blouse."

"Actually, I did." Elizabeth grinned. "You're Sally Green aren't you? Three classes behind me."

Sally smiled. "We were considered kids and stayed out of the older kids way."

Elizabeth offered a hand. "Elizabeth Turner. Afraid I'm a bit older than you."

"How can I help?"

"I'm looking for employment. Maybe in Bookkeeping or if there's something needing attention right away I'd be glad to give it a try." The red head was studying her.

"Try not to lose faith if I tell you it would be better to try out at the local gym, all I can give you here would be two days a week, start work next Tuesday." Elizabeth nodded. "Fill out the form above."

Elizabeth accepted the clip board and began to fill in the blanks.

"Wait. I just remembered there's a new business coming in from California and as far as I know they haven't hired any office personnel." She wrote the address on a card and hand it to Elizabeth. "The roads will be a bit daunting but I believe you can make it through."

She found the sign pointing to Mosby Fabricator and Contracting. Nothing left to the imagination on that title, she thought as she drove between two wood columns bearing a welcome sign. At the end of the lane stood a two story building, glass fronted with stacked cedar shake roofing and stained cedar columns. In the fading winter light it made little statement but she knew in spring or summer it would come to life, aided by its green surroundings, the metal structure and colorful roof would be beautiful.

A girl wearing jeans and a color striped sweater met her on the stairs. "I'm out for a few," she said, "But go on in and make yourself at home. Bill will be off the phone in a minute and show you around."

Elizabeth cleared her throat. "I came to apply for the job."

"Go on in, our guy is waiting for you but he'll be doing something already. I'll be along."

She thought Bill had a familiar look about him and when he laid down the phone and turned to her, she held out a hand. "Hello, Bill, I doubt you remember me. I'm moving back to Mosby and need a job." She paused, then added, "Elizabeth Turner."

Bill smiled. "I do remember you…you dated Derek Larson and left him high and dry to heal his heart."

"I'm taken back on that, Bill. I've never heard that statement before. I guess you stay in touch with Derek? How is he?"

"First, let's talk about you. You look great, Elizabeth. For what I know, Derek's doing fine."

"That's good."

"Why do you need a job? The grapevine says you're part of a big conglomerate in Chicago."

"I'd rather keep that between the two of us, if you don't mind." She wondered just how close Bill and Derek were. "As I recall, in school you were not part of the athletic crowd, you were the brain, the power behind the throne that kept their grades going. Are the school board members still as intense, you know, good grades, no sulking, keep Mosby strong and all that hipe?"

"Right on, maybe even worse and you're right I wasn't Derek's best friend but we had a general respect for each other. The coach had a hand on my ability to make good grades." He laughed. "Back to you. We probably could use your expertise as this is a new company and the owner wants to be sure we, as you and I recall, dot all I's and cross all t's."

"Who is the owner?"

"Some guy in California that sought out a small town that could use a new industry in its midst."

"Then, there will be a need for book keeping skills?" She smiled. "Do I get the job?"

"You can start Monday. Come with me, I'll show you your office."

She followed Bill. "Wasn't this too easy? What's the deal?"

"Easy for you, perhaps, but I've interviewed twenty two people thus far, both gender and it is mind boggling they would apply for a job knowing they can't spell personnel, can't add twenty five and three, in general don't have an idea what they'll be getting themselves in to and still applied for the job."

"Must not be Mosby's own."

"No, they're not. All of Mosby's own went to the big city." At the end of the hall he opened a door into a room with a wall of windows that looked out into the forest, tiled floors except where the desk sit there was a twelve foot square of carpet, bookshelves behind the desk and to the left of the desk a door." Her eyes were on the door.

"It leads to the Boss's office. I'm at the front to meet the delivery guys, you are the middle to take care of the bills and the boss… well, he said he won't be here, often…but he wanted a quiet place where he could assess the business. Don't worry; the outside has a hall that runs alongside these rooms…that door over there." He pointed. "What do you think? I know you are over qualified for the job, but…I feel we need your expertise in other areas…so can you spell and are you really good with numbers?"

"Yes, very good, I will do you proud." He was waiting for more, instead she said, "I have a question. What do I wear? The lady I met going down the stairs was wearing jeans, is that the normal day wear?"

"Actually, it's the weather, this week it's a struggle to get here, Jeannie wears what she wants. Jeannie is our go to girl, whatever you need, she gets. You will meet with delivery guys, me, and the higher ups who want a feel of whether the business will build theirs or if they should chuck this company."

"In other words, a good front is worth its weight in business?"

"Exactly!"

"All right, thanks for the confirmation on my job. I will see you Monday."

"We have all your credentials, right?" He was scanning the papers she filled out. "It doesn't have the blank filled in whether you are married, single, widowed. Is there a reason?"

She laughed. "Privacy. I'm divorced."

He marked the spot and then glanced her way as he shook his head. She grinned. "Me, too."

****

While she was out, she would run by Margie's Shop. No one was in front but she heard sound in the back. That would be Margie rummaging through bins and lid topped five gallon cans trying to make neat what had become tumbled. It never worked, but Margie stayed with it. Sweat and all.

When she returned to the front, Elizabeth was sitting by the large mannequin in the window, not until Margie'sphone rang, did she turn around and notice Elizabeth. "What live doll are you talking about?" She was asking when Elizabeth began to giggle. "Oh, my goodness. It's you. I ought to know…come here." Elizabeth stepped away from the plate glass window into Margie's arms.

"That was a genuine hug."

"It's a good thing someone called, otherwise how long would you have sit there?" Elizabeth received another hug. "My goodness, don't you look good."

"I've decided to stay in Mosby, Margie. I don't have ties to any other place. Mother said if I sold send her half, so I will send her half of what Safe Haven is worth and it will be mine. T.J. can visit all he wants. Dad left the home in the city to him, which sold immediately and the money was put in trust for his education."

"He was young when your Dad died, who did he put as guardian? You?"

"You will laugh. l thought you knew. Mother."

"She never told me and I thought I knew everything about your mother. I'm flabbergasted." Margie thought a minute. "I guess she thought I knew. We all had to admit, everything about that situation was far out. Your mother and Dad's divorce, your dad coming back with T.J. They kept the gossip in Mosby supplied for a while."

"It was traumatic, to say the least."

"Have you resolved your problem with your Mother?"

"What do you mean?"

"Lizzie, you and your mother were so close, then your dad left and it was never the same." Margie took a deep breath. "It hurts me to see the two of you closing your hearts from each other and I can't understand why it happened. She said it began the night all your group was coming in to whatever Sybil Collier called a Sorie." She studied Elizabeth. "Is there any truth in this? The night Derek was supposed to meet you and met with Catrin, instead? How could you blame your mother? Isn't that misdirected anger?"

"I have to go, Margie. I'll talk to you in a few days." She felt Margie's hand on her arm.

"Don't go, Elizabeth. I love you and I love your mother. We were friends through your dad leaving and I saw her heart ache, then you left…" Margie's voice dropped off, "I guess that's why I was surprised when she told me she saw something in that little boy she wanted to embrace…she felt you had left her behind."

"If any good came out of this, Margie, it was Mother accepting T.J. and that didn't happen over night, it was a process. Mother did see he needed love with his mother gone and she still loved Dad enough to take them in…it seemed I became the fifth wheel…"

"Really, Lizzie, when you were instrumental in T.J., coming into your mother's life?"

Elizabeth stopped abruptly. "Why do you say that?"

"She said you went to the hospital and met his mother and from there…" Elizabeth was leaving.

****

Chapter 6

"Hey Sis, what's going on?"

Elizabeth laughed. "I'm in Mosby at Safe Haven."

"Aww, I wish I was there with you. How's Nan?"

"She hasn't told you she's permanently in Florida? What do you two talk about?"

"Florida?" He sounded shocked. "I never ask. I say how you doing, Nan and how's Lizzie."

"Yeah, what does she tell you about me?"

"She says, don't you know Elizabeth is busy and doesn't call me?" He laughed. "And I say, well, she should. Then we talk about my grades and when we're going to see each other?"

"And when would that be?"

"I want to come in Christmas. Could we all meet at Safe Haven, or is that too much traveling for you to go back since you're there now?"

She didn't tell him she was staying. "Why do you want to be at Safe Haven for Christmas?"

"Come on, Sis, you know I love it. Remember the Christmas Nan had turned her ankle and we wrapped it in plastic over the boot she had to wear, so she could go out in the snow with us?"

"There's snow now. A foot deep and I wish the roads were completely clear."

"Man." T.J.'s voice was as pitiful as a little boy's when he heard Santa wasn't coming. "I wish I was there." She felt his disappointment. "What-ta you think, Sis, could we meet there for Christmas?"

"There has to be a reason mother wants to stay in Florida, if she agrees to come back, I'll get the house ready."

"You are the best. Dad knew what he was doing when he brought me to Mosby and Safe Haven."

No, he didn't she wanted to say, but she didn't and soon T.J. said good by.

****

She started the new job on Monday. Margie called numerous times but she didn't answer the phone. Every day she learned something new and in the mix was wondering about her boss. He seemed to accept her work, sending memo's to remind her of different projects he needed forms faxed to his California office. Everything had a number on it which Bill informed her was the Boss's code.

"Does the Boss have a name," she asked.

Bill gave her a strange look. "Yeah, he does but strangely, all the time he's been in California, his nic name has held. They started out calling him, Guy. I'm surprised you didn't know that."

"Remember me? I've been away eighteen years." Bill just shook his head and left her alone.

Friday rolled around, Jeanie in her denims poked her head inside the office. "You attend church anywhere, Chicago?" Elizabeth glanced up, at the name Jeannie had given her. "Well, do you?"

"No, I haven't gotten around to it, yet."

"Then I'm inviting you to Mosby's First Church this Sunday. We're having a celebration of sorts, for our pastor. It's his birthday. You want I pick you up?"

"No, if I attend I like my own wheels. You okay with that?"

"Don't forget, ten o'clock. Off Main and to the end of the street."

"I remember."

****

Saturday. After her first week at work, she tried to sleep late, but couldn't. T.J.'s request was heavy on her mind, along with Margie's opinion concerning her mother. Could it be she held resentment toward her mother, after all these years? She had tossed and turned the night through, questions rotating in her mind. The last time she and her mother were close had been the night she saw Derek with Catrin. But as she recalled her mother had stepped out to help with the event and stayed on even when she escaped saying she had an upset stomach. Still as her mother comforted her that night, she learned Nancy Ann had known without sharing the information, her father's affair was with a young woman barely older than his daughter. She thought if there was resentment it lay with his choice of leaving his family for another. Her anger had been with Derek and Catrin. She pushed it away, and went on with life…or did she? Now her world was unsettled as tried to figure out at this late date just how did she feel? Right now, however, she needed a hammer to hang a hook in the closet. She had not seen Derek since that night. Losing their friendship had wounded her more than anything, before or after, but now try as she might, she could not analyze the situation considering the years. She left for Chicago when the Firm showed interest in her. Either you went immediately or you were passed over and those were associates with her father. After graduation there was a place for her. They felt she had learned from the best. Her father.

Her marriage was not in Mosby's elite section of the newspaper and she asked her mother not to talk it with her friends. "Let's let sleeping dogs lie," she said. For once, her mother agreed. And if anyone knew she was divorced, she could handle that. She was a lot stronger as a woman than she had been as a girl. She was told the community thought T.J. was her child. "Who cares?" She asked her mother. "I don't."

"Well, I claim him as my grandchild," Nancy Ann replied. "So let them figure that one out. Sometimes you don't add fuel to the fire, you just let it smoke."

Now, T.J. was twenty years old. She imagined the tongues that wagged were gone.

Going to the basement to find a hammer, she opened the door where the Christmas decorations were stored…and that was a whole new world. Dragging plastic containers from the closet she began to remember where her mother had placed the wreaths and the garlands and then there was the first artificial tree she'd bought, "Because I'm tired of the fireplace drying out the needles on the real trees," she said, "we could burn the house down." The box said nine feet, but when they assembled the look-a-like wonder it was mislabeled and was twelve feet tall. They had to relocate it to the one place the ceiling was high enough. Because of that location, Nancy Ann had the wall between foyer and living room taken out and now only a six foot half wall at the door divided the two. Funny how she'd forgotten that.

Forgetting the hammer she dragged the smaller containers upstairs and went to work. When she finished small wreaths were inside the windows with a strand of lights beneath on every window ceil. Outside large wreaths hung with bright red bows. The column posts were wrapped in garland and a huge wreath on the door. "Just like you did it, Mom," she said.

"All I like is the twelve footer, but I'm tired." She chuckled, talking to herself. "Well, there's no one else, so tomorrow after church I'll tackle that big box and hope I don't twist my ankle like my mother did." She fell into bed shortly and unlike the night before when her dreams had been troublesome and the hours of actual sleep few, tonight she slept.

Still, when the alarm sound the next morning she awakened, startled to think she was late for work, but reason flashed inside her head. "Oh, thank goodness, I'm attending church."

******

She didn't remember the church lot being as full of cars and trucks as it was this day. She parked in the business lot across the street and went in.

"I'm sorry, Miss," the usher said, "We're having a special celebration today, we've just about filled every seat." He began canvassing the rows, "ah, yes, there's an empty seat by John Larson. If you don't mind pressing by two other ladies to reach it?" He led her to the row and she began the process to reach the vacant seat.

"Well, hello," Mr. Larson greeted her. "My name's John and who are you?"

"Just call me Elizabeth," she replied, accepting his hand. "Glad to meet you."

He showed no sign of recognition, which was a relief. She tried to settle down to enjoy the singing and then there was special music where she recognized Bobby Dugan at the piano and all those years past flashed through her memory of him complaining he was probably the only boy in Mosby whose mother made him take piano lessons. Now, she understood why. His talent was obvious.

She realized she would not be able to tell anyone the pastor's message, so caught up in old time memories, they had consumed the whole hour. When Mr. Larson turned to her at end of worship and ask, "Young lady are you staying for the fellowship dinner? You are very welcome to join us."

"Oh, no, Sir, I didn't bring a dish and I would feel like an intruder."

"Don't you live here?"

"Well, yes, but I'm new to the community."

"Come with me," he said, offering an elbow for her to slip her arm through. "You can be my date."

She found herself laughing. "You are very gallant and I appreciate your hospitality."

She heard his voice as he pressed through the people in the aisle, "Come on, old friend, Come on, step out here, I want to show you to my family." Bobby was taking her hand and leading her to the front of the church. "Elaine," he began as he introduced his wife. "Honey, this girl, right here, was the third party of my friends through school." Elaine reached for her hand.

"I feel like I know you. Bobby's friends from growing up seem to live in our household. Did you ever make a mistake? Because when I hear about you, you are perfect. I wish I was."

"A figment of his imagination, Elaine. I assure you."

"You must join us for our little celebration." She saw Elizabeth's hesitation. "You must." She laughed. "We will protect you. There's always an intimidation, isn't there, returning to old places."

****

It was three o'clock when she let herself into Safe Haven, with a glance to where the tree would stand, she had to take a few minutes to rest. The Pastor's celebration was fun packed with many people she recalled from child hood and a few, like herself that didn't know

97

anyone. The food was delicious. She really must work on her cooking skills if she planned to attend that church. With Bobby and family there, it would be easier and she already knew she liked Elaine.

"I'm one of the liaisons for the new business in town," Bobby confided. "I took this job as Music Director knowing the salary would not meet my family's needs. The member body made it clear I could find other employment." His smile was filled with mischief, "with three kids, you know I must."

"What do you do for the company?" She smiled in return. "I'm the new book keeper."

"Really? Well, it will be good to see you around. I drum up business, contact established business in the area and explain how Mosby Fabricators can help them." He sighed. "There's a misconception what exactly we can do. We work with all materials and our employees are highly trained craftsmen."

"Do you like the Boss?"

He gave her a strange look and she remembered Bill doing the same. "Well, yes. What's not to like. He runs the business through his employees here, from his office in California. I doubt he'll move back for this company when he has others there. I think this one was established to help an otherwise dying community. Our people were all leaving to find work in the city and Mosby was hurting."

"It's always nice to know if your new boss is a good guy or if you must be constantly on your toes."

"He is fair, but astute."

"Then you have met him?"

"Yes."

******

At work, more than once she heard Jeannie refer to her as Chicago. To keep the record straight when she faxed the boss she signed off, Chicago. Life in Mosby was different; where in Chicago she worked at a fast pace, lived life accordingly and was always wondering if it would let up, here in Mosby she found most people's social life centered around the church and the church seemed to promote some kind of get together to celebrate their very existence and eat.

"Is eating behind every activity in this little town," she asked Jeannie.

"Yes, ma'm. We love food. I'm glad you noticed. So what dish will you take next week as we open the Christmas Celebration?"

"Christmas Celebration? And that includes what?"

"Oh, there will be one night a week we go caroling, another we meet to play games to teach our children it's not all about materialistic gifts but what we give to each other in time."

"I didn't know you have children, Jeannie."

Jeannie dissolved into laughter. "I don't but I do have the age seventy group of ladies and gentlemen In our congregation that I take care of. I love them to pieces; they span the whole gamut, fun like children, wise like Paul and sometimes as cranky as all get out."

"I know you are good at it. You certainly have a handle on what's needed here before we even ask."

"Thank you, Ma'm. I appreciate the compliment. Put that in the box for Guy when he comes."

"The Boss? You mean he actually makes an appearance?"

"Yeah, sometimes when we least expect it. I bet Bill didn't tell you that so you wouldn't be anxious."

****

The next Sunday Mr. Larson was missing in church. Elizabeth sit in the usual pew but she missed him. There was something about the old gentleman gave her a peace and calm to carry through the week. Maybe it was his wonderful voice, she often caught herself listening, or perhaps it was the prayers he offered up when the Pastor called on him to pray. He truly seemed to know the Lord. Whatever it was, she hoped he would be there the next Sunday.

On Monday Bill called her in to his office. "There are a number of forms needed for this particular business," he said. "I'm expecting a new customer in, and these numbers have to go to a merchant here in town, do you mind running them over? This will give you an opportunity to get acquainted." She nodded. "The address is here, on the shipping labels we supply, but before you go brush up on what is expected of the client and specifically what is expected of Mosby Fabricators." He smiled. "The owner can be a bit testy. Remember you are our person representing this business." She turned toward the door. "You did this very thing with the law firm, right? There's also a mock up of our new invention you can leave with them.

"It's not heavy?" He shook his head and motioned her out the door as he answered the phone.

She took thirty minutes to read the company by-lines and then studied areas in which the client must comply to be accepted for orders. If the owner was testy, perhaps she should view the model she was delivering before she opened the box in front of him. At first what she was viewing made absolutely no sense. She studied the name of the object and then decided to try it out, first locking the outer door. Well, yes, she decided, she had a handle on the item and repacking it was on her way.

"Mr. Harwell," she said, extending a hand, but Mr. Harwell only grunted. "I've brought the sample for item number three five seven eight that you requested. Would you like to try it, before I go?"

"No, just leave it on my desk and be on your way."

"Sir, I'm bound by contract to explain the procedure to use this item and either I show it to you or you will have to bring an employee in that I might explain it's important the user knows the correct adaption, meaning it cannot be turned the wrong way to receive relief of a hurting joint."

"Aren't you a bit old to be playing doctor? I understood you were the bookkeeper. Right?" Mr. Harwell stood." What can you know?" Elizabeth didn't bat an eyelash. "All right," he practically barked.

"Let's get on with it."

That's when she saw he was having difficulty pushing his body up, with the use of his right arm hanging nearly useless by his side. Immediately she glanced around for a flat place large enough to lay a body, hers or Mr. Harwell's. "Sir, would you happen to have a conference table handy?"

Mr. Harwell snorted. "Now, what are we playing? Office?"

"No, Sir," she said with kindness. "The item of the month is designed to help those who have degenerative arthritis, or a torn ligament or possibly an out of socket, dislocated shoulder where the arm has become detached and needs the comfort of being aligned for sleep which can be a miserable time when it happens to you. You want to sleep but there's no support for the arm and the body aches to the point one cannot rest. I don't know if you've ever experienced such, but I have."

She smiled. "You know what I did this morning? Before I brought this little miracle to you, I locked the outer door so no one would think I was foolish if they found me and I placed this item on the table and climbed up to put my shoulder in it and just see if it worked…and I can tell you, it works."

"What it does, is takes the weight off because that's what's pulling things out of place, this is like a Miracle. I think you would understand what I'm trying to explain if you would try it. The relief is instant."

She gave it one more try. Mr. Harwell was not biting. "You know, when we have aches and pains we become very protective of ourself. Well, I decided, those people around me deserve better than me growing anxious or nervous due to my own shoulder that was injured in a car accident, if I can relieve the pain during the day by giving up, say fifteen or twenty minutes using this device, then I will be nicer to my people and hopefully they won't have ugly stories to pass along to other people."

"Well, Sir, I have to get back to my desk. I'll just put this proto-type back in its box and proceed to the office. I certainly would love to see what you think about the item. Thank you for your time and the papers I was to deliver are here, on your desk. It was nice meeting you."

"Hold on," Mr. Harwell replied." I believe the office next to us has our conference table. Just follow me." She followed and watched as Mr. Harwell reached the table, backed up to it and swung his body onto the table. "How's that?" He asked.

"Perfect," Elizabeth said, beaming. "Now." She was wearing a sweater set and removing the outer sweater rolled it up for Mr. Harwell to have a pillow under his head. "Now relax," she said. "Just breathe in and out. Allow your body to release any pent up tiredness from not sleeping last night. That's good. Now I'm going to place the item under your right arm to allow the burden of weight to dis-tribute. This new device is normally used after a required surgery has been done or in the event a patient is seeing a chiropractor and they've not eliminated the problem where sleeping at night has major discomfort." She saw the ease register on his face, those nasty deep wrinkles were dissipating.

"What do you think?" She asked.

"I wouldn't have believed it," he said. "Young lady, you are a dang good salesma…woman."

"You can thank Mosby Fabricators, Mr. Harwell, those engineers work closely with doctors and patients. I thought it worked wonderfully."

"Did you say you were in an automobile accident the reason your shoulder suffers at times."

"Yes, Sir, that is correct." She was reclaiming her sweater and smiling as she prepared to leave.

"Say, what is the name of the item?"

"Exemplar," she called back. "Yes, Sir, the Exemplar." Oh, Lord, she prayed help me through this."

****

"How did it go?" Bill was waiting. Mr. Harwell was the company's most obstinate client. He always purchased for his medical supply company but it was like arm wrestling an alligator. He doubt this lily of the valley princess was able to get through to the old goat. He did not voice his opinion. He was waiting. The phone rang before Chicago could answer.

"Mosby Fabricators. Yes, Sir. Well that's wonderful, Sir. Yes, we will. You have a great day, also." Bill stared at the phone as though something might jump out and bite him. "I cannot believe that." Now his eyes held with Elizabeth. "That was Harwell. He ordered two hundred of the Prototypes, but he called it the Exemplar." He saw her head drop to her chest as his eyebrows arched. "What does that mean, the Exemplar?"

"He wanted a name. Exemplar means prototype. I'm sorry. Do you want me to go back?"

"I'll have to think on this one, Chicago. Just go on to your office. I'll let you know."

Had she been a child, Elizabeth would have tucked her chin against her chest the rest of the day. She felt bad about misleading Mr. Harwell. He wasn't so bad as they said. He just needed attention. Little did she know, Bill was laughing his head off. When Jeannie returned from lunch she ask what's so funny. He couldn't tell her.

The clock on the wall was striking three when the door opened. Bill glanced up. "Boss?" He rose quickly to his feet. "I had no idea you were coming in. How are you? Let me pull up a seat."

"It's all right, Bill. Gramps is in the hospital. I came by to pick up those papers I text you about. Where do I go to meet the new girl?" He frowned. "Did you say she goes by Chicago?"

Caught completely off-guard, though it didn't matter as he had done no wrong, Bill wondered how Chicago would fare with this one. They were on their own. Both were adults. He pointed down the hall. Guy was on his way. In the beginning Bill thought they were once an item but maybe not.

Chapter 7

There was a book shelf with a dictionary behind her desk. Maybe she should check out the meaning of Exemplar before they hung her. Who did she think she was naming anything? She wasn't that important to the company. She was new, for heaven's sake.

She heard the door down the hall open and close and someone was moving around in the room next door. For the first time she felt nervous. True Bill was easy to work with, until today. She was a lawyer, for heaven's sakes. What made her name the device? It was crazy. She turned around to reach for the Dictionary. Running the alphabet she found e. Define exemplar. There it was. Exemplar. Enough already. She felt someone standing in the room with her, just beyond the desk. They came from the Boss's office. She turned around.

"Derek?" She didn't know if she felt pleasure…or something else. The last time she saw him, he was with Catrin. Puzzled, she asked, "Is there a reason you are here? Did you want to see me?"

He was rooted to the spot, his eyes locked in a definite questioning glare. "Who are you? I mean I know who you are but what are you doing here?"

"I work here."

"What do they call you?"

"Who are you? I mean, I know you are Derek but what are you doing in the Boss's office?"

"Wait a minute. I have to check something with Bill. Stay. I'll be right back." His steps thundered down the hall. "You want to explain that person sitting in the office," he turned, pointing, "there?"

"You don't know her?" Bill's mouth was gaping open. "I thought you said you did."

"Aren't you supposed to tell me when you hire someone to this office?"

"Yes. And I have. I mean I did. You have been corresponding with her on a daily basis."

"Who?"

"Elizabeth."

Sick to his stomach Derek slumped down into the chair opposite Bill. "I didn't know I was. I thought I was talking with someone named Chicago. She sent all the papers, all in order, everything fine but there was no Elizabeth."

"Didn't you two attend school together? Weren't you as the grapevine gossips said a thing?"

"She stood me up."

Bill's mind was racing, trying to catch up to what his boss was saying.

"Do you hear me?" Derek's voice raised and Bill made a quick glance down the hall.

"Do you want me to fire her?"

"You don't have to." Elizabeth came out of the office, her coat on, with a plastic container that held all the favorite things she had placed on the desk, even her own lap top. "You have my address, Bill. I quit."

Derek was pointing like a tattle tale kid, "She stood me up after all those months."

She stopped in front of Derek. "For the record, I didn't stand you up. You came in with Catrin and you were having so much fun you didn't see me. It made me sick to my stomach. I went home."

He rose up to meet her head on. "Oh, but I did see you and by the time I climbed the stairs to where you were standing you were gone. Disappeared, just like the plans we made and I thought about every night for six months. Poof." He blew into the air, his fingers stringing invisible bubbles to where she stood.

"And then, you danced all night with Catrin."

"What was I supposed to do? After I came to your house and beat on the door and you wouldn't let me in. Yes, I danced the rest of the night with Catrin and did I have fun? No, not until I was drunk."

"My point, exactly. It hardened my heart. If I couldn't trust you for one part, then I certainly couldn't tie my life up with you."

"Ha. I heard you did exactly that. You allowed your husband to treat you terrible. You held one night dancing with Catrin against me and then you lived a lifetime with a man who treated you worse."

"I cared. Don't you understand? It was hard to let go because I cared so much, but you, you didn't care, you left me."

She knew. She truly realized she was acting like a high flying narcissistic bitch, but what he did was the beginning of her settling for less in order to show him there was more to life than a man who cheat on his girlfriend. "I've heard all I need to hear."

"Go after her, Derek. You wouldn't have fought so hard if you didn't care and you said some horrible things."

Derek's eyes came around to Bill. "You have no idea what you're saying, so shut up."

Bill turned to his desk, picked up his brief case, grabbed his sweater on the way out and was gone.

He had never in his life seen Derek lose control as what he had just witnessed and they operated by a strict code, you didn't tell someone you were in business with, shut up or curse them out. He must still love her, otherwise the hurt would not sting so deeply. Bill went home to Madeline and was glad.

The next morning he groaned as he rolled over in bed. He'd slept tense as a fiddle string, not knowing if he had a job. Whether to go in to work or not was the question. His phone dinged and he read the message. "business as Usual." Derek "I apologize."

"I don't look forward to this day, at all," he told Madeline.

"Why?"

"Because yesterday a mad man took control of my office." Madeline laughed.

******

Derek's car was parked on the side of the building. Bill found the phone ringing. Derek was answering. It quit ringing around eleven o'clock and Derek came out of his office carrying a hand full of order slips. "What in the world is an Exemplar? Do we carry it? There's orders from all the main medical companies we supply and they all said Mr. Harwell had called and recommend it and as hard as he is to please it must be good." Derek laughed, good naturedly. "I had no idea what they were talking about but I did take the orders."

"An Exemplar is a prototype of the new device one of our engineers fashioned to help people with certain types of Arthritis, certain needs following surgery, it goes on and on…but the name…well, they didn't come up with the name…it was spawned out of necessity…Mr. Harwell's need as I understand."

The phone began to ring again. "What?" Bill laughed. "I think you need to talk with the company CEO. Yes, he's right here, Mr. Derek Turner." He hand the phone to Derek, "they said they are an equal to Shark Tank. They're interested in your new invention."

"We need a Secretary," Derek reminded Bill. "Someone to keep this place running."

Bill rolled his eyes. "We had one. You were mean to her and she quit."

"She had it coming."

"For something that happened twenty years ago?"

"Eighteen."

"Give me a break." Bill found himself walking down the hall to Derek's office. "We're swapping," he called back. "I have work to do and I'll be much slower since we don't have a girl Friday."

Derek followed him down the hall. Clearing his throat he said, "My things are in there."

"I won't bother them."

"I'm the owner. I think I have priority over my office."

"You did, until you fired the best secretary I have ever had, okay quit looking daggers at me. You were going to fire her but she beat you to the draw and quit." Bill let that sink in. "Your actions mean, that left you responsible for answering the phone and since we've hit pay dirt on a new little device, I assure you there will be a lot of calls and a number of orders. Good luck." He tried to shut the door, but Derek's foot was in the way.

"Really?" Derek's eyes were narrowing. "Call her back and tell her I acted on impulse and I said I was sorry."

"I have a better idea. You were going to fire her so you call her."

"I can't." He turned to go to the front. "All right, I acted in haste, I made a mistake. You call her."

******

Bill called from the Boss's office. She picked up. "Chicago, please come back to work. We don't know how to do any of the stuff you do."

"Your boss was out of line." She replied, her chin sitting in a ferocious way. "Let's just say a cold day you know where will happen before I give him my time.

"It was his idea for me to call you, so I'm asking you to come back."

"We worked well together, Bill, but you know what it takes for me to come back."

She heard Bill's deep intake of breath. "Bye, Elizabeth."

She began to think there was no need going to the basement for the tree. She had lost complete interest in anything festive for the holiday. If T.J. came home and wanted to, they'd do it together. She thought for a moment whether her brother would like Derek. Today, she doubted he would. Another time, she might have said yes.

Margie called. "Hello, Sweetheart, where have you been? I thought you would come back to see me."

"I will. Sometime this week."

"How's the job going?"

"I guess that hasn't gotten out yet. I walked out, Margie. It was too much for me."

There was silence on the other end of the conversation. "Honey, that don't sound like you."

"It is. I'm pretty discouraged."

"Come sit with me tomorrow. I've got some fellow coming to help me pull fabric on a big old sofa, but other than that I'll be workin' around the table. Pretty much in this one room."

"You don't know of anyone needing office help, do you?"

"I only know of one place needing anybody to work and that's the Country Club."

"Waitressing? I haven't done that since my first year in college."

"How's the decorating coming along? And don't say you've not started because I know you have."

****

Elaine called the next morning. "Elizabeth. Jeannie told me a little bit of what happened. Would you like to meet for brunch? My kiddo's will be in school. I can be at the Edge by ten thirty if it works for you."

"I'll throw on some clothes and be there," Elizabeth replied. "I have nothing more to do."

"So tell me about it," Elaine said. "Bobby heard a little of it and he said never in his life had he seen Derek behave the way Bill and Jeannie described it. By the way, Jeannie hid in the closet. She said she was afraid to come out when they got your name mixed up, she was afraid they'd blame her."

"I'll go back to eighteen years ago, maybe a few months more or less, Derek and I were young and thought we loved each other but we attended different colleges and it was time for the annual school reunion and I was waiting for him when he drove up with Catrin Collier. In those days, Catrin seemed to take away everything that came my way and I guess that night I got tired of it. I was instantly sick at my stomach and I ran; all the way to the car and home as fast as I could go. I haven't seen him since that night getting out of the car with Catrin and walking in with her on his arm. My life was pure misery for about a year and then I met Addison."

"Whose Addison?"

"The man I was married to for seventeen of those years and Derek was correct, Addison led me a fool's life. I was the fool. I allowed it, one woman after the other and then he left me completely."

"Why did you allow him to treat you that way, Elizabeth?"

"You don't allow it, it happens. A man with a loose foot doesn't know how to stop running. He loved the chase and conquer bit with women. I doubt he enjoyed any after he caught them, but he wouldn't quit."

"Could it be you still loved Derek?"

"I was blind sided by Addison's good looks and his attention in the beginning, so I think I loved him enough but Addison never loved anyone but himself." She took a deep breath. "I don't know, Elaine. I'm messed up over this. I came back to Mosby to start a new life, to put all the drama behind me and find peace. Look what blew up in my face today."

"Have you felt any of the peace you were searching for, since your return?"

"Strangely, I have. But the office fiasco is a bit of a set back. There's very little comfort." She crumbled the paper napkin laying by her silverware. "I feel humiliated, like everyone's talking about me behind my back and I wanted to be through with that."

"Jeannie may have told Bobby and me, Elizabeth, but otherwise I'm thinking loyalty prevented it going farther and Bill is a friend to Derek."

"You don't think the whole town's talking?" Elizabeth lift her head to see Elaine's expression as she shook her head. "I would feel better if that's true." She placed the silverware on the opposite side of her plate. "Something else bothers me, Derek said he had stayed informed of the way Addison betrayed and treated me. I don't know why he would do that."

"Maybe he still cares." Elaine held Elizabeth's stare. "Bobby said he never gave up on you. I know there was almost a time he almost… but did you know he never married?"

"No," Elizabeth's voice was barely above a whisper. "I squandered my life, Elaine. He didn't."

"Life is not over," Elaine said gently. "This time next year this heart ache will be forgotten; You will be happy and going forward. Life will be good."

"Is that a prediction or a promise?" Elizabeth's voice broke. "I could use something good."

"Listen, I've got to run. We're working on a women's weekend at the church for next May and this is our second meeting. I think it's going to be fantastic. Could I enter your name for a committee?"

"Maybe if I'm here, next year, I feel a little unsettled presently. But thank you for having faith in me that I could do something."

"Oh, honey, I see ability written all over you and great control. You didn't wipe the floor with Derek."

They laughed together and hugged and Elaine was gone. It was nice, her encouragement. Elizabeth thought of her mother and suddenly wished she was with her and they could just sit together.

****

"No, No, Nooo." She awoke to the clock's alarm singing its silly little verse from childhood. "We work, we work, we work." Slapping the clock, she pulled the pillow over her head. It was her intention to stay home, in case anyone heard about her job prob, as she had come to think of it. She was not going to church.

But she couldn't go back to sleep. She tossed and turned, tried to think of something pleasant but in her mind all she saw was Derek's face wrapped in anger, his eyes casting blame on her and his voice, that terrible voice that said, "you ran away and left me. All I've ever known is being left and you were the one person I knew would never leave me."

She remembered things about Derek he had probably forgotten, how he always seemed to draw buildings as they listened to the teacher's lecture and she wondered when he would get caught. "I listen," he said, "but I also draw things I want to remember while I listen. What's wrong with that?" She always thought he would be an architect, and maybe he started that direction and was deterred. It didn't help she knew the story. It was true. His family abandoned him, except for his grandfather. Had she ever said she would never leave him? Yes, but she had no way of knowing there would be Catrin's in this world.

Self blame attacked her. Rebellious nature defended her. "How could I be guilty of all that when I was twenty two years old and why is it bothering me now?" The voice on the right shoulder spoke to the voice on the left. "because all these years you have been sorry for your rash actions. You ran and somewhere in there you wish you hadn't." The left replied, "perhaps she only wondered if things would have been different." To which the right replied, "There's a way to find out, throw out the white flag, surrender and see if there's a chance to find out what might have been and then we will all know."

"Enough, all ready." Elizabeth realized she had tried in half-sleep to work through the situation. Grimly awake now, she muttered, throwing the covers back, "all right, I will get ready and go to church and see if there's anything to your argument. In frustration she glanced up to see her expression in the mirror. "Not good, is it, talking to myself over some little creature on each shoulder?"

She dressed with care, her make-up, the gray set of clothes that appeared elegant but on this down-cast day she added a colorful scarf that brought out the color of her eyes. Shoes. How could she have forgotten the gray alligator shoes? She had the purse, but the shoes were missing. She hurried through her mother's closet and found a pair that worked, if they fit, and they did. Now she must hurry; she had lingered too long with those little devils on her shoulder....well, maybe one was an angel.

The usher's face lit up seeing her, placing his hand lightly at her elbow to walk with her to the usual pew where she sit beside Mr. Larson. "Here we go, John's back from the hospital. He won't tell you," the usher leaned in close to her ear, "He had a Urinary infection, nearly knocked him off his feet. I'm the one found him, took him to the hospital and they kept him. He was a bit upset with me, you know. I called his grandson in from California." The usher, a Mr. Beecham, according to the name tag, left her laughing as John gave him a dirty look." The look was not missed. "He's back." Mr. Beecham gave her a dazzling smile and left her in John's care.

"How are you, young lady?"

"I'm very well. I'm sorry to hear you've not been well."

"That's kind of you," John Larson replied, "I'm pretty much back on my feet. It's good to see you again." He glanced to his right, an empty seat. "My grandson will be along to sit with us. Even though its Sunday he felt he had to check in at that business of his. Seems they lost their Secretary and he's trying to fill the slack." Suddenly he gave an embarrassed laugh. "For a minute there, I forgot. You know my grandson, Derek, don't you?"

"Yes, Sir, I know Derek." She smiled. "Anyway, I used to know him."

"Good. Good. Good." The music began, with Bobby at the piano as Mr. Larson reached for a hymnal. "I love the old time hymns," he whispered. "I've noticed, you and I enjoy singing."

"Yes, we do," she replied, reaching for her own book and opening to the page Bobby announced.

It was during prayer with heads bowed and eyes closed she felt someone slip into the seat next to John Larson. In glancing down she saw tiny flecks of black on the floor. Concerned, she studied her shoes, one seemed larger. Could it be? Dismayed, she realized she had a real problem; the shoes from her mother's closet were old and though they looked new they were falling apart. Just her luck. The last song was sung and then the sermon began and as usual she found it hard to concentrate, with her shoes falling apart in despicable chunks and the owner of the business where she had worked before her job-prob, sitting on the other side of an innocent John Larson probably seeing it and enjoying it profusely. Her thoughts were not good. How was she going to keep her pride, clean up the mess of her mother's shoes and hobble out to her car with any dignity at all? She could just cry.

The Pastor was welcoming the people, the people were greeting those around them and finally settling down to the scripture of the day as the pastor took his place and began to speak.

"Today, our scripture will be two-fold. I was thinking about the ladies of our church making plans for the annual women's presentation and I ask Elaine, who is in charge, what the theme would be next year and she said, encouragement; Encouragement, because we live in a world where women must handle so many different situations in the lives of their spouse and children and they need encouragement. "Be strong and courageous, do not fear or be in dread of them, for it is the Lord your God who goes with you. He will not leave you." Deuteronomy 31:8. "We are using that scripture, too," Elaine informed me, "But we are basing our theme on Titus, chapter 2."

"Now that's good. Titus is such a small book of the Bible, but there's more packed in those three chapters than we can imagine. Yes, three chapters. For instance, it tells women to be self-controlled and pure." He laughed. "I don't know about you fellows, out there, but in my household with three kids running every direction, a wife that's pure and controlled is an asset. That being said, I leave The book of

Titus to the Women's Gathering next year and today we will concentrate on Deuteronomy 31:8.

"What happens when the best laid plans fall apart? Often there's blame, whether self-blame or casting the problem on someone else. Now, the Bible cautions us, tells us to restore not only ourselves back to fellowship but to the other person. It also warns us to put away falsehood, to speak the truth.

That passage is found in Ephesians 4:25-32. But that's not where we're headed. We are seeking the word for the time we are just so discouraged our feet are dragging. Have you been there?"

"Have you found those situations a waste of your emotions, a waste of your time and later you couldn't believe that you were sitting there all beat down, your shoulders slumping, your spirit defeated? That's what we need to work on as we turn to Psalms. Chapter 42:5 asks the question, Why are you downcast, O my soul? Why are you disturbed? Yes, asking a question when not two chapters back in Psalms 40:1-3 the writer of this passage tells us, "I waited patiently for the Lord; he turned to me and heard my cry. He lift me out of the slimy pit, out of the mud and mire, he set my feet on a rock, He gave me a firm place to stand, He put a new song in my mouth, a hymn of praise to our God. Many will see and fear and put their trust in the Lord." Let us take this a step farther and ask our self, have we been in this position lately? Discouraged or upbeat. Encouraged or defeated?"

Elizabeth, brought her eyes to the minister. Was he speaking to her? No doubt he spoke to a dozen or more in the congregation. She was pretty much beaten in her spirit concerning the job-prob and the reason was sitting on the other side of John Larson, who no doubt had no idea the problems he created.

For a minute rage burned high, and immediately she felt the war being waged within.

That's not quite what the pastor had in mind? Oh, no, she was mentally shaking her finger. You two do not surface here. We are in the Lord's house. Not your territory. The one on the right was shaking its head and clapping hands, while the one on the left was complaining what would happen next. She almost jumped, glancing around to see if anyone noticed. She hoped she didn't drift off; surely it was a reaction to her being in deep thought. None the less, she was happy when the sermon ended.

There was the usual song and then it was time to leave. Almost hopeless, she turned to Mr. Larson. "Sir," she leaned in close, whispering into his ear. "I've had an unfortunate thing happen. I've noticed the door to our right. Does it lead outside that I might use it to go to my car. The sole to my shoe is literally coming loose from the leather." He was glancing to her feet and then her worried expression. "I'm really embarrassed," she added, "but I'm afraid walking in it could really ruin the floor."

"Of course, young lady. You can go out that door. I'll see to it. Come with me." He spoke to his grandson. "Derek, I'm going to escort this young lady outside; I'll catch up with you in a minute."

She and Derek ignored each other, with Derek stepping to the next row to be immediately claimed by two of his grandfather's friends. He was aware that Elizabeth had stooped down to remove her shoes and that intrigued him even more as to why she and his grandfather were leaving by the side door.

"Excuse me," he said to the two, "I believe my grandfather may need assistance." But the door had closed and they were on the other side. Derek headed for the front vestibule. He would catch up, except for the congestion. Mentally, he shook his head. What in the world was behind Elizabeth removing her shoes and how well did she and his grandfather know each other. He was beside himself with curiosity. Of course she would play the part of the victim if she confided and told their story. Bill said he over acted but he didn't think so. He couldn't let her get by with a repeat performance; it had angered him considerably that she considered Catrin on his arm that night a reason to sever their relationship. Through eighteen years of dissecting that one night he concluded she was wrong and it was he who paid the price, forget that he did have Catrin on his arm, it was Elizabeth he was anticipating seeing and Elizabeth he loved, had loved these eighteen years and thought it was his opportunity to tell her…but they had gotten off on the wrong foot. Again. He was behaving like a school boy in love for the first time.

His grandfather was nowhere to be seen. He went to his car and waited but John Larson didn't show.

He's eighty years old, he reasoned, just out of the hospital. Where is he? Becoming a bit antsy, he wondered whether to go back inside the building or wait. What if he went home? He saw Bobby Dugan's van coming his way, it looked stuffed full with Bobby's kids in the back.

Seeing Derek, Bobby stopped even with his car. "Looking for Gramps?" Derek nodded. "I know he was escorting your old flame. Why don't you come home with us and have lunch? If I was him with that good looking woman I'd take her somewhere for dinner." Bobby laughed. "Maybe that explains his absence." There was side chatter and then Bobby added, "Well, leave it to the little woman. She met up with the two walking the side of the church building and invited them to dinner. Seems your Gramps was speaking with Nell. She probably ask him where he was going. Anyway Our house. You never know about these women. You coming now, or not?" Laughing, he added, "It's a challenge, isn't it?" Shaking his head, Bobby drove away as Derek's phone dinged. He read the text. "Derek, this is Nell from church. Your Gramps said to tell you he will ride with Elizabeth to Bobby and Elaines."

It was a challenge. Derek's head was messed up, running into Elizabeth after all the years since he heard she married. He had been curious as to his replacement and hired a friend to check out the marriage. What he'd learned, was disturbing. Her husband had several affairs but she had lasted a number of years longer than he'd thought possible. Elizabeth wasn't one to give up on a husband if she thought things would get better. He wished she would have had that trust in him. Maybe they were kids in those days and maybe he had taken her word to heart too soon in life. Maybe that was why he'd gone off the deep end that day…realizing she had made commitment to someone else while he waited all those years. Had they really changed that much? To find her and lose her again opened the wound.

****

"Mr. Larson, do you mind if I swing by my house for a pair of shoes that aren't falling apart?"

"I'd enjoy seeing where you live. They won't have food on the table for awhile anyway."

"It will take just a minute," she said. Once there, she hurried and was back in different shoes.

"Mr. Larson, I was wondering, do you remember me?" They had walked to her car together, and discussed whether to continue on to have lunch with Elaine and Bobby. It was his opinion people did not invite you if they didn't want you. But they had not discussed whether he remembered her and she questioned whether he made any connection between her and Derek "I decided to ask you, as I've been wondering since the first time I attend your church and sit by you. If you don't, I understand because it has been eighteen years."

"Well, that's one reason I asked Nell to let my boyo know I was riding to Bobby's house with you."

"That relieves me a bit," she replied. "I didn't know if you told him where you are going."

John Larson laughed, his gentleman way, "When someone comes that far to check on you, you do. He's my boyo and he worries over me." He gave her his quaint gentleman smile. "But now, we've been sitting by each other at church awhile and I want to know you, young lady. I have thought you were the one Derek was so intent about before he went off to school, but then there was that other one." He fumbled for the name, trying to remember. "Cat? The rich people's girl."

"Yes, Sir, that would be Catrin."

"What kind of name is that?" He shook his head in a trying to understand way. "Couldn't they have finished it out, you know made the spelling complete?"

"Catrin's mother told my mother that it means someone special. She is an only child."

"I'll take your word for it. She showed up at my house once with a far out story and I sent her home."

"That's interesting."

"No, it was actually a sad story. Forgive me if we drop the subject. No need raising the blood pressure."

They arrived at Bobby and Elaine's. The pastor's car was already parked but Derek's wasn't.

"Young lady," Mr. Larson said as they stepped onto the path to the house. "I believe my grandson has kept an interest in you. I'd like to see him happy. If you have any interest in him, then I welcome that but I'm asking you not to tread on my boyo. His life was always people leaving and he needs someone to stay for a change. If that's you, then think what your next step might be but I'm asking you to tread lightly. Take time."

So, Elizabeth thought, his riding with her had a reason, not some far-fetched plan of an old man. John Larson was an intelligent person with his grandson's happiness uppermost in his mind. She didn't know how she felt at the moment. She had considered coming home to Mosby the beginning of her own. Why wasn't life simple, they could leave off putting themselves through the turmoil. That was the crux of the matter, wasn't it, time had possibly changed who they were and they must find each other again.

Church seemed to have set the tone. She and Derek avoided each other. Bobby kept trying to bring them together and it was embarrassing. Dinner became a fiasco of forced laughter as Bobby sought to reunite them. Finally, Elaine asked, "Elizabeth, do you want me to call Bobby off?"

"Yes, please." She replied with a deep sigh of relief.

"He's the ultimate romantic." Elaine grinned. "I suppose that's what drew me to him and by the way, he has told me some of the best stories of what the three of you did together as children. That's one reason we came back to Mosby. We could make so much more money elsewhere but this little hidden town is great for raising children."

There was one mention of something she had not known, when she overheard Bobby whisper to Derek, "it's true, there was a time Catrin looked pregnant, then she didn't and her mother was raising a child, next thing we hear the child was adopted out. It interfered with their social life. Yes, if it's true it was cruel." She was stunned. She hadn't thought even the Colliers that heartless. Surely it wasn't true.

Elizabeth found her mind in a quandary, ready to leave, hugging Elaine and Bobby and their busy children before taking Mr. Larson's hand into her own as she said goodbye. "I didn't mean you had to ignore him, young lady," John whispered in her ear. For a moment

Elizabeth had to think what his words meant and then she laughed self-consciously, glancing to where Derek stood talking to Bobby.

"We are at an empasse', Sir. I don't think you have to worry about us seeing each other. We are history."

"Well, now, don't bet on that," he replied. "I really like you, so I've added you to my prayers."

John watched her walk away, glancing to where his grandson stood. The boy had always wanted a family. This girl seemed worth her weight in gold and a glimmer of remembering her teased his mind. "Lord," silently his thoughts went to the Lord. More and more he was leaning on The God of salvation, the one who had been with him when the love of his life died, when his own son left him with a child to raise and even then he was labeled frail, but God knew what frail meant, sometimes he thought it meant one thing had been taken but another placed for constant use and that was strength, the kind of strength that relied on the Lord. "Lord, bless that young lady and if she and Derek got anything in common bless that too."

Chapter 8

On Monday Elizabeth decided she could not stand herself a minute longer. On a lark she headed toward Mid-Valley's Country Club, that hallowed shrine frequented by the rich and famous, except there weren't that many rich or famous from Mosby. The Collier family, for sure, and then the rich Daddy's who were imports that wanted their sons on the Basketball team that won, because they paid a coach with the most skill to lead them to victory. Nothing had changed.

She filled out the application, taking in the atmosphere and a hope of expectation by the cook.

"You don't look like a waitress," the cook said, who was also the owner and manager of the Club.

"Really? You don't look like a cook. What's the deal?"

"Cook had an accident and is laid up with broken pelvis and spine. May never come back." He smiled, motioning she was to follow him. "I got potatoes cooking on the stove. Real potatoes, not the kind comes out of a box. Anyway, couldn't find a cook, tried it and I like it. I got tired buddying around with the boys knocking those balls around. Some of them are terrible, couldn't hit a basketball."

"Where's your waitresses. No white table cloths, nothing set up to serve. What's that about?"

"Probably got beat up last night, one of them. Stella's husband gets drunk, takes it out on her." He saw her flinch and wondered about it as he glanced at the tables still holding the chairs they'd placed on top when they swept the floor. "Cindy on the other hand. Who knows, car ran out of gas, flat tire, her brother borrowed it. You name it, I've heard it."

"So, are you hiring or was this drive out here a wild goose chase?"

"Look, you even talk citified. Why would I hire you?"

"From the looks of this run down place, how could you justify not needing me?"

He spread his arm wide, "Knock yourself out. Show me what you can do, then I'll tell you if I need you."

"Point me to the necessities and I'll make you proud."

"It's a joke, right? Someone sent you out here to harass me. You're just another rich dame."

"If I were, I'd be sitting over there in the corner watching you, maybe I'd be doing nothing."

She found the white table cloths, and the silverware and prepared the tables, sitting a small vase containing one artificial sunflower in the center. After inspecting the silverware she returned to the kitchen, dumped the mass into a sink she filled with hot soapy water and asked, "who in the world washed the silverware. I wouldn't touch it and I doubt your dinner people would either."

"That bad, huh? I hired a kid to do that as the dishwasher is broke."

"You want to be sued?"

"What would you know about that? Being sued is the last thing I need."

"Then you better get the dishwasher fixed." She heard the crunch of tires on the drive as she glanced at the clock. "Isn't it early? Eleven seems a bit so, to me."

"Nah, if you're going to waitress, help me set the food on those two tall tables, I had to go tall to keep people from leaning over the food, now it's near their bent heads and they don't do it anymore."

"We haven't introduced ourselves. I'm Elizabeth."

"Joe." He studied her "that sounds too above waitress status, We'll call you Lisbeth, or Lizzie. You choose. She picked up a magic marker and wrote her name on a name tag, Lisbeth. "Okay," he said, "now you and I step back and watch the food disappear."

"There's the problem. Where's the drinks and the glasses I would think also need to be on display."

He laughed. "Maybe you have been a waitress once or twice but don't ask me about the girls. I don't know." He was enjoying her company. "I'm trying to figure out if you will wear the above knee skirts and the low cut white blouse my waitresses wear. What did you really do in life?"

"I was a lawyer." Joe's eyes bugged out.

"Then what are you doing here?"

"It's called boredom. I got tired of me…heard you need help. That would be me."

"You got a place to stay?" His eye was on the three seating themselves at the first table. She nodded. "You're hired. For now, anyway. Do I really need to get the dishwasher fixed?"

"Don't mean to scare you but salmonella is a very serious complaint from restaurants. The health board gets involved and it ain't pretty." Their attention to the clientele became necessary when a group of fifteen or more came in, laughter lighting up the room as Joe backed behind the counter and then hurried to the kitchen. The dinner guests were filling three of the round tables.

"Lisbeth, is it?" A familiar voice sounded almost sarcastic as she turned with the notepad ready to take orders for drinks. Derek wore a mocking expression as he held the chair for Catrin to settle in.

"Why hello, Elizabeth, I didn't know you were back in town. Fancy meeting you here." She smiled up to Derek. "I don't remember seeing you since graduation." She placed a hand on Derek as he sit beside her, while the rest of the group were happily eyeing the buffet. "Was that high school or college graduation, Hon?" Derek was as loving as a man caught in a snare replied, "I think college but I don't think you saw Lisbeth."

Everyone at the table laughed as Derek sounded tongue-tied saying the name. She kept her cool, but inside she was seething. "I don't know any of your friends," she said, smiling, "but it's good they enjoy your jokes. It always seems small to me when people find pleasure in another's discomfort, so it is good there's no one here that does." The friends seemed to swallow their laughter.

Ever one to have the last word, Catrin asked, "How's that boy you had right after we graduated College?"

"Oh, did you think that was my child, Catrin? I was wondering if the grapevine had the story right about you having a child? Was it true? Or another one of those things you tried to hide? Or maybe give away?"

Catrin's face went white. "Who would tell such an ugly vicious lie?" She hid her face in the white cloth napkin. Derek on the other hand had stood abruptly. "That was uncalled for."

As equally annoyed and quite truthfully ashamed, Elizabeth smiled and turned toward the kitchen. "I did something terrible," she confessed to Joe. "You may want to fire me."

"I heard," Joe muttered. "Don't even think of quitting. Catrin plays her cards both ways. Just watch." He flipped a fish patty in the skillet. "I take it you knew her before. Well she doesn't change."

Catrin had very little to say to her after their first trial run of setting facts straight. She noticed the friends left a sizable tip but there wasn't one cent by Derek or Catrin's plate. Raising her eyebrows, she showed Joe the tip, he nodded. "Kill them with kindness and ignore their barbs, is my advice."

"I'll take your advice. I doubt we see Mr. Derek Turner here again."

"I wondered about him and what he's doing in Mosby. Could tell he wasn't a regular."

"No, he's here from California, he owns the business on the back road. He'll probably go back…"

"How did you know him?"

"We both grew up here and played together as kids until Catrin got in the way."

"Why do I sense there's more to this story?"

"I don't know, is there something wrong with your nose?" They laughed together. "Well, your waitresses didn't show, does that mean I have a job?"

"If you want it, but a dame like you, educated, knows the ropes, tell me why you want it?"

"Don't want to travel outside Mosby presently. I will enjoy meeting regular people. It beats sitting in an empty house wondering what to do."

"I hope you don't regret it. Isn't it something, the two before you didn't have courtesy to even call?"

She made the trip up the hill to the Club every day surprised the crowd was growing and she was wrong on one thing, Derek Turner did come to the Club more often than she would have anticipated. He hadn't returned to California. It was said he was bringing all of his business back to Mosby. His product would sell from any state and was doing very well. She did have a brief moment to wonder how the Exemplar was doing and there were times she wished they were still friends when she caught him in the middle of gazing her direction as if he was trying to understand what she was doing there.

Few people would understand when a woman lived under the thumb of a man who flaunted women in front of his wife for no reason as though daring her to do something about the situation; it was heart breaking to the point of destroying her spirit. When he began to drink more often and couldn't hold it, he became abusive. The doctor said, "he could kill you." She had to leave or go down in the rubble.

Joe was fun to work with. One day he said, "I'm having fliers printed. You have a new title, you are not the waitress. You are the hostess, as if you are entertaining from your own home. How do you think that will go over?" He was smiling.

"Are you serious?" He was nodding. "Hey, I may have to throw away the white apron." She did a little jig. "I might wear a black dress, even. You know, a little black dinner dress." His smile widened.

"You know, Joe, you are a handsome man, even more when you smile. Why don't you have a wife?"

He spread his arms wide and ask, "do I look like I need one? For the record, once, I had one."

"Aren't you lonely?"

His laughter had a rebuking tone to it. "I'm surprised you, of all people, would ask. Tell me your story."

"Handsome man, charismatic to others, I couldn't understand what happened between us, we both changed. I wasn't one for the life style of being with other people every night, the drinking and all that which led to other women fawning over my husband and he liked the attention, I did not."

"Look at you now, working in a club where the elite hang out. Were you jealous?"

"No, I was tired. I needed time to focus, keep my mind on what was needed in court. I could not keep up with his life style…then there were the nights he didn't come home, pictures in the paper and people not looking me in the eye because they knew things I didn't…" "So you lived a life more lucrative than most of us here in Mosby?"

"Let's just say we didn't want for anything…but things aren't what make you happy, are they?" They stared at each other a bit, lost in their own thought. "Your turn," she said.

"Have you seen my home?"

"No, I actually wondered if you lived here. I saw the back room. A bed, television, all you need."

"Yeah, it served its purpose when my wife was doing about the same thing as your husband. I go home now. She left and took her boyfriends with her." He sighed. "She had an itch I couldn't scratch. He changed the subject. "How are you handling serving that Turner guy? He comes about every day"

"I can't figure why. What do you think? He sits there and stares at me, moody or judgmental, I haven't decided which. I try to push him out of my mind."

"Difficulty doing that? Pushing him out of your mind?"

"Yeah, something like that. We had some good times together. But we were young." He was chewing his lip as if he wanted to say something. "What? Go ahead. I can take the criticism."

"Not criticism. I'd say go after him if you still care…but then I know there's Catrin to deal with."

"You know her?" At that moment the lights went out. She glanced at the clock as it went down.

"Ten thirty. What do you think that's about?"

An hour passed. Joe couldn't cook, the building was getting dark inside and cold.

"Come on," he said. "Let's get out of here. Your house or mine? I've got a fireplace with wood stacked beside it ready to go." He grinned. "There's an old crank Victrola, we can fire it up, too, a little cheese and crackers, a bottle of wine…you're not against wine, or you? If you are…there's…"

"Tea. Hot tea. How does that sound?" She was removing the white apron and putting on her coat. "I want to see your home, anyway. I don't have wood ready to go in my fireplace."

"Just take the road around back, through those trees and we are there. It's Mosby's best kept secret. The community knows it's there but no one bothers. Get's their vehicle dirty." They were riding in her Jeep. "See what I mean?" The home came into view, a sprawling ranch with a stone wall on each side and a drive made from same. Tall pines circled behind and the view was spectacular.

"You weren't here when we were kids. How did you do all this and my mother never mentioned it."

He pointed beyond the stone wall and tall trees. "An outter road leads to the Interstate, so all the materials to build came from that direction, as did the builders who live in the next town. Like I said, for the most part it was Mosby's best kept secret."

"I haven't even seen the inside and I can tell, either you or your folks have money. Rome wasn't built in a day and this …this is beautiful and so well done. Tell me about your family." She was following him to the huge oak stained door with iron hinges, into a foyer that spoke as highly of skilled craftsmen as the outside. "You don't have to operate the Club, do you?"

"No, but what would I do with myself? I like people, so I consider it a service, of sorts to the community. They never welcomed me into the circle so I made my own and they just appear."

Elizabeth's laugh was joyous. "I'm so glad for you, happy to see you enjoy this and a part of me is a little jealous. Your parent's raised you right."

"But not here," he replied. "My dad was a doctor, Mother begin adulthood as a teacher, met Dad about the time she became a

Professor teaching College classes and they had me. Dad was fifteen years older than Mother and when he retired they came here away from the hustle and bustle…truth is, we were happy until I gave them a few aches and pains caused by my being spoiled and needing to learn a lesson or two I didn't think they could teach me. I had a wild spell…that cost us dearly."

He was turning the handle on the Victrola, music poured into the room, as he lit a match to the tinder and soon the room was warm. "Let's raid the refrigerator," he said. "I actually made chili last night."

"You are a wonder." It was the first time she had seen him without the apron. "Why, Joe, you work out don't you? No beer gut, just a six pack to brag about. But you don't."

He lay the knife down by the cheese, came toward her with his hands in the air. "May I have this dance, Madam?"

"Certainly, Sir," she replied. "Who are you? Prince charming in disguise? Sir Galahad?"

"Just Joe," he replied as the music ended. "Now for cheese and crackers and hot tea for you."

"And chili you made last night. Thank you for this lovely respite from work and boredom."

"You're quite welcome. We have only the light from the fireplace and I apologize. I've been intending to get a generator, but I'm not here a lot and I keep putting it off."

They ate in silence. When finished she said, "I had three cups of tea. Where's your bathroom?"

He pointed. "Down the hall and to the right. I'll close up the cheese and crackers and then we can decide if its dominoes or checkers." He called down the hall as she left, "wholesome entertainment at its best, wouldn't you say?"

"Down the hall and to the right," she muttered, going through the first door, but it was a bedroom. "He must mean beyond this," she stumbled in the dark and a door opened, his bathroom she supposed as the fragrance of aftershave lingered. Searching her pocket she brought out her cell. Maybe there would be signal…but at first it didn't light up and then seeing not only the commode but the wall over the tub, a life size painting of a woman, not completely nude as there was a long sheet that covered most of her body but still left much to see in that shadowed light of the cell. The face was hauntingly familiar and yet she could not see to study the features enough to know who it was.

She was back in the hall when the lights came on and to her left was an open door to a bathroom, no doubt the one she was supposed to use. Hurriedly she stepped inside, flushed the toilet and was back out to find him at the end of the hall waiting for her.

Glancing at the phone in her hand, she said, "Joe, I need to go home. I've been here over two hours."

The lights blinked and were gone again. "I guess that's my cue to go home and see if I have electricity.

Time just flew by."

"I know, but it was nice. I'll ride with you and get my wheels, if that's okay with you."

They arrived back at the club to find a group gathered around the door, trying to see through the windows. "Are you closed?" One of the men called out as Joe climbed out of the Jeep. "There wasn't a sign on the door."

Joe laughed. "Yeah, we're closed. You can't see your hand in front of your face in that building, when the electric goes out. That's why I didn't hang the sign. Sorry."

They began to leave, one by one, watching where the stepping stones rose a little higher in places. Someone's car lights came on and

Elizabeth recognized Derek's car. Then she saw him, watching her, a strange expression on his face. She felt a hesitation, as though he would say something, but he turned to where his car was parked. The lights came on just as Joe pecked a kiss on her cheek.

"Goodnight Lisbeth," he was smiling as he closed the door more firmly and left her.

She drove home, lost in thought but once she glanced in the mirror to see a car several lengths behind, almost as though it was trailing her. A crazy guess popped into her head, could it be Derek, but he had made it clear how he felt about her. She dismissed that idea. She was still caught in the web of mystery concerning the life size portrait in Joe's bathroom. You had to care about a person to hang a portrait of that size. It wasn't a caricature, more a dreamy impression of a beautiful woman and she felt she knew that woman.

The phone was ringing as she entered the house. "Hello, Darling, how are you."

"I'm fine, Mother. And you?"

"I'm minding my manners dear. I'll be home for Christmas. Have you decorated?"

"I started but," she took a deep breath, 'I got sidetracked and I haven't finished."

"You have to focus, focus, focus. Your brother called and said he is coming in. Won't it be grand?"

"I suppose. Would you have even made the effort if T.J. wasn't coming in?"

Nancy clicked her tongue. "Darling, that is just too childish coming from you. Of course I would."

"It's supposed to snow."

"I'll bring my boots. Anything else?"

"No, the rest will be here." She swallowed and continued, "By the way, I may be working part of the time."

"Did you open a practice? Tell me about it."

"No, sometimes I open a buffet; sometimes a bar and sometimes I just do whatever's needed."

"What does that mean?"

"Do you remember the club just in the beginning edge of country as you leave Mosby?"

"You are not involved with the Belieu establishment, are you?"

"It's possible. Is there a son named Joe?"

"Joseph? I thought he left. You know his wife broke his heart and when her family gave their child away that was the last straw. He went into a deep depression, locked himself away from everyone and everything for years. How did you meet Joseph?"

"I'm his waitress." Nancy Ann was very quiet."

"Be careful out there, Darling, things are not always as they seem."

"I'm his waitress, Mother, not his love life."

"Thank God," Nancy Ann replied.

"Well, are you going to tell me?"

"Can't. Gotta run. Talk later." The house line clicked silent.

There was only one person might know the rest of the story.

****

There was a glimmer of light between the blinds at Lettie's. Using her phone as a flashlight she hurried up the sidewalk and knocked on the door. 'Who is it," came the muffled question. "Just me, Elizabeth."

Lettie pulled her inside. "Girl, what're you doing out in this mess, and no one with power. I declare, it's dangerous out there. So let's sit over here by the fire and you tell me why you're here, because

135

you wouldn't be out if it wasn't important to you. I heard the club closed at noon."

"Oh, you did? What else did you hear?"

"Doesn't matter. I'd rather hear it from you." She settled back to listen. "Go on. It's your time."

"What do you know about the owner of the Club? When did he come to Mosby?"

"Joe Belieu?" A kind of protective expression flit across Lettie's face. "Joe Belieu is a good guy with a bad past. By that, I mean there were troublesome times, but he never hurt anyone."

"Who said he hurt someone, not me."

Lettie laid a hand on Elizabeth's. "He was accused of hurting someone but it just wasn't true. I know."

She let Elizabeth think on that sentence. "When it all happened, I was actually doing upholstery work for his parent's home, where Joe lives now. Did you notice any of my work on all those pieces of furniture?"

"Truthfully, it was dim; even in mid-day and we were too busy eating cheese and crackers and he had made chili." Raising an eyebrow, she continued. "He excels as a cook and as a hostess he is superb. The home appears to be a master piece put together by skilled builders. You've been there?"

"Yes, it is and Yes, I have been there. I met his parent's, both very educated and then there's Joe."

"You are smiling, almost grandmotherly over Joe? So, what's the story of his coming here?"

"As I understand, Joe served in the Marine's. He and a group of his peers were sent out in one of those, what do they call them, Amphibious tanks, the kind that are let down on the ocean floor and travel the distance to shore, unseen, and then just come up out of the water and there they are." She took a deep breath, "and that's what was supposed to happen, but something went wrong and they all died, except Joe and he couldn't accept it at first, he hit a low. Depression and trying to forget his friends dying and not understanding why he alone was left were the undoing of a fine young man."

"He never married?"

"Not exactly."

"Either he did or he didn't, Lettie, there's no not exactly, is there?"

"Maybe sometime there is. His parents had The Club. Sometimes he helped out, other times he became one of the diners and that didn't go well when he drank too much, his personality changed."

"You can't watch a grown man all the time and he was a handsome devil with great charm. You know that…and there was this one young woman attracted to that charm. Naturally she made a play for him and it worked…she caught him and he was like a fish out of water with her; head over heels in love."

"Wasn't that good for him?"

"Under some circumstance, perhaps. But not always, when you choose the wrong girl."

"Why didn't I know about this?"

"You were busy getting ready to go off to college and then you did leave."

"Is that when it happened? Mother would have told me."

"Yes, if you were speaking to her. Think back, you were anxious to get away."

"No, I wasn't. At that time I was dating Derek, I was sad we were going to have all those miles in between and Catrin threw another problem into the midst, suddenly she was going off to college where Derek was. I could never figure that out. He said there were a number of months she wasn't even there and then when she came back it was as though she was angry with the world, with him and her parents who were at home in Mosby. At least I guess they were. No one told me different. It was after I graduated college and ready to study with Dad's law firm that we kind of had our disagreement, because Dad called me when Sarah was dying and that didn't go over well with Mother."

"Yes, all things have a beginning, innocent as they may seem. Then you didn't want to come home. For a year or two you were filling in Sarah's absence, weren't you? Your Dad did come home and bring T.J. for holidays and then on the last all of you seemed to get in synch, pulling together for your dad, loving the little boy who is now twenty years old…"

"But why didn't I know about Joe? Did I know and can't remember?" She sighed. "A lot was going on back then and it was a real trauma Dad dying, even though the doctor warned us he only had two years to live…" She held Lettie's gaze, "What else? Joe said he had a wife who led him through about the same as what happened to me and Addison. His words were she had an itch he couldn't scratch. What was that itch if he did fall in love and marry someone, was she from here? Did I know her?"

Lettie grew quiet. "Sometimes, Elizabeth, good people decide not to participate in hurting another."

"After Catrin did everything she could to break up me and Derek, it was even more difficult to find each other again. There were always those images in my mind of them and I already had to adjust to Dad being away from us and then seeing him with Sarah, maybe I did find it hard to let go, such as the time Sybil Collier organized what she called the Soiree', what happens? Catrin and Derek arrive at the reunion together and after that I didn't see Derek again, nor have I spoken to him until the day at work."

"Maybe you should. John Larson once told me, first his mother left, after a while his dad chose a lady whose name was Jenny and Derek became close to her and she left, and then his daddy rode out of town leaving his little boy as though Derek didn't count. John said it left a stigma on Derek. He believes all his people leave him." Elizabeth sat back down, her eyes not leaving Lettie as she listened.

"We can't say Catrin left him, Lettie. If I saw her today, I believe she would flaunt Derek in my face."

"There will always be Catrin's, Elizabeth. We have to decide to ignore them but pay attention to the Derek's of this world. I understand he's made a name for himself in his line of business."

"I thought for a minute you were going to say he was wealthy. We both know money doesn't always mean a stable life, sometimes it's a means to have more than your neighbor and that's not happiness."

"Sweetheart. You seem tired. Go home and sleep on whatever is bothering you today. Tomorrow has to be better."

"I will." She hid a yawn behind her hand. "I wanted to know about Joe, but I see you won't tell me."

"We all agree to let bygones be bygones, Sweetheart. Will it help matters if I tell all I know?"

"It might help, Lettie, if I knew about Joe and maybe even who you think Derek is with now."

"Those who knew agreed to silence on the subject, Elizabeth, in order not to hurt those we care about and I can tell you it was a growing experience for all of us because those who hurt, hurt deeply."

"Meaning Joe." Elizabeth yawned. "I get that but mother warned me not to go out there and Joe in explaining his family said something…let me think how he said it. "He said, I had a wild spell that cost us dearly. He was speaking of his family." She tried one last time, for information. "What does that mean?"

"Before the divorce, Joe's divorce; there were rumors his wife was caught with another man, Joe's friend, to be exact. Joe went off the deep end. He loved his wife, although she didn't deserve it, she had his child but that didn't go well with her family's social life, a baby needs care you know. Either the the child was sent away or put out for adoption, maybe even whisked out of the country. Joe's family wanted the child but spite played a huge part in the wife's family and I suppose that is what Joe referred to, grieving the loss of that child his mother died and within a year his father. From what I saw the father was a good number of years older than Mrs. Belieu. Does any of this ring a bell?"

"Yes, it does, for the most part but there's still the mystery why mother said be careful out there."

"There was a restraining order. Joe was not to go around the ex-wife, but I don't know how long a restraining order lasts. Still, I was told the ex would go around him just to antagonize him, or could it be in some sick way she finally realized she loved him? People do strange things when they are in love and just want to see that person."

"Lettie, you are describing other people and I'm wondering if there's some of that in you?"

Laughing, Lettie replied, "Well, Sugar, if there is I need it slapped right out of my head, but on the other hand you might wonder why Derek Turner remains in town. There has to be a reason."

"Let me clue you in on that," Elizabeth's expression was resurrected from her past career. "One. Mr. Derek Larson is obviously enraptured with Catrin Collier, whatever her name is now. Two. He has an elderly grandfather that needs him near. Three. He always planned to build a business in Mosby and spend his last days here."

"Ha. Did you say end or spend his last days? He's what? Forty years old, if he's a day. Still not married. I remember that lanky boy that worked here the last summer before college. He was head over heels in love with you."

"Not any more. I'm out of here, you're no fun. I have to drag info out of you. Goodnight, Lettie."

She let herself out into the cold, with Lettie's words ringing in her ears. "Maybe he still loves you."

Banks of dirty snow lined Main; the landmarks were now visible and the sign pointing toward Derek Larson's place of business was visible. For a moment she wanted to turn that direction, just to view the building as she knew it would stand, enshrouded by frozen limbs as the lamplight made the ice sparkle like diamonds. Whoever designed the building made it an asset to Mosby that was already compared to a vintage village of the past. She had missed that and when the longing to return became a part of her dream she thought of Lettie's shop and Marge's boutique. Two very successful business women, she could exist among them with no shame, only pride that she was a home town girl.

She was so involved in thought she didn't see the low slung black car half hidden behind the bush. She was startled when the door opened and Derek slid out, coming to take her elbow to lead her up the path as he spoke, "Hello, Elizabeth. I've been back in Mosby long enough to visit and you let me in, don't you think?"

"Did you have to scare me like that?" She gave a firm thrust that bent him sideways as he tried to correct his balance and keep from falling. "Hmmm. Did I almost cause you to fall? Mercy, we don't know our own strength. Why are you here?"

"Elizabeth," he was quite put out. "Can't you be civil a minute. What's happened to you?"

"People like you and your cohorts, I guess." She spread her hands innocently. "Who knows?"

They were on the porch when he asked, "Are you going to ask me in?"

"I don't know. I'm waiting to see."

"I want to talk to you, seriously."

"Seriously." She laughed, not the most genuine or convincing. "Whatever about?"

"Us."

"There is no us. That was years ago. Now, we are adults." She tried to put the key in the lock. His hand was on hers, taking the key.

He was successful, the door opened. "You need to change this for the push number kind."

"It's all right."

"Until a burglar comes up behind you and takes the key away from you; with the other you would already be in the house."

"All right. So we are in. What is it you have to say that is so serious?"

"May we sit, please?" He sit on one end of the sofa, Elizabeth on the other. "Listen to me, don't turn me off, I remember you were very good at that."

"Not with you," she said insulted. "Had I known the future, I would have."

"Elizabeth, we can't go on like this, ignoring each other, hardly speaking, our friends waiting for the next insult."

"I didn't realize it mattered, especially to you, you're always with people and seem well attended."

"What does that mean? Well attended?"

"Look, you're the one came here. What did you have in mind?"

"Come back to work. Take your old job."

"There's something missing, I believe a stipulation."

"I'm sorry I insulted you and intended to fire you and you beat me to it. You quit."

"I have a new job."

He gave a gnarled laugh. "What? As a waitress?"

"Wait until your next visit to cast doubts."

"Will you come back?"

"I would have to leave early in order to be on time to my other job."

He groaned. "What is your schedule?"

"It depends, if Joe finds someone to fill in, I can leave at two for your office and work three hours, or I can come at six thirty and leave ten thirty and still be Joe's hostess. Not that it matters but the evening hour is when most folks come for dinner and I must be there. For Joe."

"Are you two…"

"NO," she cut him off. Her eyes snapped. "Are we finished? I'm ready to go to bed."

"You are so different. I can't get over the change. Where did the sweet girl go I fell in love with?"

"She took in to consideration how deceiving all the nice boys were until they turned into…" She stood. "This is ridiculous." She walked to the door and opened it.

He was almost out the door when he turned suddenly and took her in his arms, and she stunned found herself eyes closed, helpless to move not sure she wanted to, as his lips were on hers and Derek Larson was kissing her and she wasn't quite sure how it happened but it did and once he finished he walked out onto the porch whistling, stopping to turn, "I'll be calling for a date. Think how you will handle my call. Don't hurt my feelings."

She slammed the door, leaning against it as if the strength had left her body. She heard his laughter.

He sounded happy. Was she imagining things?

******

Her teeth had never had such a cleansing. Adrenalin was flowing. As tired as she had been, now she couldn't sleep. The covers on the bed were pushed aside, the pillow pummeled again and again until finally she climbed out of bed, walked through the house seeing something out of place here and another item there, the floors needed sweeping and the carpet vacuuming. She did them all.

The nerve of him to kiss her after the last weeks of confusement. She ground her teeth, chewed her nails and continued dusting the house, rearranging this and that on the table tops all the while staring at the spot where the tree normally sit but that was the one task she would not undertake.

It was three o'clock in the morning before she finally fell onto the bed thinking she might sleep. The dreams came, enticing, unbelievable. She was in a garden, wearing a long white dress and carrying a bouquet of pink roses, waiting for someone and she felt immensely happy. But a woman was coming toward her in such pain Elizabeth could not stand it. She knew that long red hair as she turned toward the woman ready to console, leaning out to give her the roses, the woman raised up the hood to reveal her face. "He's my husband you know that, so leave him alone. Completely alone."

Elizabeth awoke. She knew that voice, that face. It was Catrin Collier. The man was Derek Larson.

Chapter 9

It was Sunday again. Church day. Weary and blurry eyed, she tried to think whether to go or stay home. If she stayed home it was another long day and she needed the scripture to carry her through another week. Shame washed over her that she and Derek had fought like teenagers these last weeks. For Heaven's sake, she was trained to stay calm. Why had he gotten to her when hardened criminals and trained lawyers could not? What was the reason?

She dressed, careful the shoes were her own, a pair of light gray whether they matched or accented what she wore no longer mattered, she could not leave black chunks of rubber sole on the church carpet. One always prompt and on time, today she lingered to allow Mr. Larson and his grandson to be seated. The usher offered his arm and she walked down the aisle, seeing Elaine on the side waving at her. She mouthed the word, hi, and walked on, but Mr. Larson was sitting on the inside and as big as life Derek was standing, a perfect gentleman, but she refused to be seated between the two, taking the end.

"Good morning," he said and she gave him a cold squint eyed look as the first hymn began with everyone standing. Derek offered to share the hymnal with her. Next to him Mr. Larson was singing his heart out. Almost, she smiled but Derek was watching. "Let's sing," he said, as though they were seniors in school and would receive a better grade for the effort. "Amazing Grace, How sweet the sound that saved a wretch like me, I once was lost, but now I'm found, I was blind but now I see." His voice rang out, as powerful as his grandfather's with as great a sound. The second verse began as he held the book in front of her. "Stop." She whispered and he laughed, placing his right hand across to help hold the book as he placed his left in the small of her back for the third verse and then closing the hymnal as the pastor replaced the Music Director for reading of scripture.

Don't we look compatible, she thought, with murder in her heart. "Let not your heart be troubled," the pastor was reading from the Bible. Later she would realize they lasted through two additional songs and the pastor's sermon was beginning. All the while she was growing more tense.

"Unbridled, Unnecessary and Useless. That's the title of today's sermon. Now some of you will listen because you need this and others are already turning me off. What are you thinking this sermon is about? World Books? Because we have the net. We can look up anything. The list goes on, needless things but this is about something we are all capable of…we all do this…and it never helps matters. I'm speaking of anger. Unbridled. Unnecessary. Useless." He waited for the usual sigh to cross the room.

"Whoever is slow to anger has great understanding, but he who has a hasty temper exalts folly." She heard Derek laugh. "Refrain from anger and forsake wrath. Fret not yourself, it tends only to evil. And here is the best one yet, But you O Lord, are a God merciful and gracious, slow to anger and abounding in steadfast love and faithfulness."

"Do you see what we can have if we leave anger out of the picture. Steadfast love and faithfulness."

"What if this was your last hour and you were angry with someone and had an opportunity to set the record straight, apologize and give forgiveness where you thought a wrong was committed? You make the decision. You leave church. You enter the Interstate…and then it happens, an eighteen wheeler cuts you off, your vehicle slides under the wheels of that massive vehicle and your life is snuffed out. That's a bit drastic, but it could happen. I'm not really sure why the Lord laid this sermon on me this week, but I assure you, someone sitting in this congregation knows why. Precious time is being wasted when precious joy could be found, someone has the opportunity to increase in steadfast love and faithfulness to the Lord and what is given will return fourfold."

"Think about it," the minister was saying as she slid out of the pew and started the long walk toward the usher who had led her up the aisle to be seated by Derek. Now he opened the door for her exit. Driving home, her thoughts were scrambled. What could she do to release the anger and anxiety? It was too cold to take a walk but she changed into the heavy clothes that had hung in the closet for years and pulled on the heavy rubber boots she found in the utility room.

No one had walked the path to the tree house. The snow was without dent except where birds had made a trail. It crunched beneath her feet. She was winded when she arrived to wipe snow from the board plank bench. She sit to contemplate what the minister said. Was it true, she wasted energy and time holding Derek accountable for the night of the huge school reunion, when he was with Catrin?

If she thought she was miserable under Addison's thumb while he paraded his latest ladies before her, she had been doubly miserable after Derek came to town. Why? Because should she run into Derek she hoped to at least be friends. Just because she loved him in their youth had nothing to do with now. It was time to resolve the animosity so unlike her that had sprung up between them.

She hadn't known Derek owned where she was employed, nor why Jeannie labeled her Chicago. Not in her wildest dreams had she suspected Derek Larson was her boss. That was another thing; the dream. It had left her shaken. To think old friends disliked her that much. It was Catrin in the dream said, "leave my husband alone. He's mine." It was a dream she chided herself. Surely he was Catrin's husband if she had a child. Nothing made sense. Why did Catrin pale when asked if she gave something away? Why did Derek say it was beneath who she was to say that…whatever his words, he had been terribly angry. She spent considerable time on that one. Why was he angry?

Life is fiction and fiction is life. The old saying claimed her as she tried to figure it out. She couldn't ask Joe because of what Lettie had told her, except Lettie evidently didn't know Joe's wife, since the Belieu's moved in to Mosby, during the time Elizabeth's group went away to College.

Funny, the scene hadn't changed, twenty years since she'd sit here and yet it was the same. She had changed. She left a carefree girl, a bit worried she couldn't handle what she left behind but anticipating a future. Meeting Addison had seemed a good thing but his insecurities were more than she could perceive. He drank trying to cover them up and he partied with women. "I can't change," he said.

"Only if and when you want to," she had replied.

Addison had been out of her life long enough if she wanted to date another man, she could. Did she want to? Addison never treat her with the kindness and patience Derek had. The hurt seeing Derek and Catrin together had cut deeply, hadn't he ask her to never leave him because everyone else did? Yet, she left Mosby after seeing him with Catrin. She realized now he couldn't help if another woman had laid wait for him, but he had fallen too quickly, giving her pause to think. The truth was she didn't know if he cared for her. Lost in thought, cold and shivering, she sat there on the bench, wondering what she must do.

"A person could freeze out here." She knew his voice and turned slowly. "It hasn't changed, has it? He sit down beside her. "I thought

I'd find you here." He glanced around. "Nothing's different. Except us. I don't know about you but I have a lot to lose if we don't get this problem that's reared up between us resolved."

"What can you possibly lose?" She wanted to say, "Aren't you the rich guy with everything?"

"I lose a dream I've had for eighteen years, of coming home hoping and praying one day you and I would meet back in Mosby and you would let me explain what happened the night of Mrs. Collier's big Alumni gathering."

Words to the minister's sermon pricked her conscience. "I know I'll hate myself for asking but what did happen?"

He scuffed a toe in the snow, settling back into the bench. "We were at the same school and she was adamant she must ride home with me and I wouldn't say no, I thought I could handle her. But she had been drinking and it got worse as we neared home. I was to pick her up that night. The rest is history."

"I don't understand. I'm the one saw you two dancing together and I'm the one who was standing in the balcony watching when Catrin slid against your body and you kissed her. The other thing is you were not in your car. It was Catrin's."

"I was to pick her up because she had been drinking but when I went out the door, she was sitting in the driveway waiting for me to come out and she would not allow me to drive. I was concerned because she had been drinking all the way home. Her parents had purchased the new car because she left the old one at school. Did you know she had a new car? I didn't until she came to pick me up."

"No, I ask whose car it was and my mother said Catrin's. But that has nothing to do with what the whole world saw out of the two of you. I had waited months to see you, but the intimacy the two of you revealed out on the dance floor was enough for me to know I was not going to subject myself to the ridicule of our peers. God knows I had enough ridicule with what my father put us through."

They were quiet, each thinking their own thoughts. "I'm cold," she said. I'm going back to the house."

He rose up, putting his hand out to pull her to her feet and walked beside her as they had twenty years before. "May I come in?" He followed her in knowing her disapproval.

"There's really no reason for us to discuss this further, Derek."

"Is it so terrible, Elizabeth that you won't forgive me and let us get to know each other again?" He leaned forward, intent, staring into her face. "It's been twenty years, Elizabeth. Give me credit, I never married. What I felt for you and the disappointment of what happened, through the years I seemed always to get cold feet. It wasn't fair to the other person. The truth is I never felt as deeply for another woman."

"Then why are you always with Catrin?" She motioned for him to sit opposite her.

"That's something I can't go in to, Elizabeth."

"Then we have nothing more to say." She stood. "I'll see you to the door. I'll be civil at church but I don't think I will return to the business. You must quit thinking we can have some kind of relationship. We can't. I've been through a marriage that failed and that was enough. I don't need a man, a boyfriend, or a husband especially one that keeps secrets. I've learned to take care of myself."

"It's a lonely life, Elizabeth. Believe me, you reach a point you want someone to call your own. You of all people should know that."

"I won't. I've made it this far, I can make it on my own." She opened the door. "Goodnight, Derek."

"This is the second time you've shone me to the door, Elizabeth. I'm determined we will make amends. For Heaven's sakes, it's been twenty years." His frustration was showing. "Can't you bend a little? What has happened to you that you are so unforgiving?"

"Tell me about Catrin and I'll bend." She watched him stalk off the porch.

"I'll be back, Elizabeth. This has to end. I didn't stay here, or move my business back for nothing."

That is your clue he does care, the angel on her shoulder reminded. She was certain the one on her left was asking, "are you going to fall for that?" He's like the knife salesman, will say anything. She couldn't wait for the next day to arrive, to go back up the hill to the Club and hopefully find a clue to the identity of the portrait in Joe's bathroom, maybe he would know the story everyone was hiding about Catrin. Whatever it is, I wish there were people that loyal to me.

Now that she had successfully run off Derek, the question taunted, what will you do this afternoon. She picked up the phone and dialed, "Lettie, what are you doing?" She listened. "Come on over. It's your turn."

She heat up the chili Lettie had made, found crackers and cheese and made fresh tea. The table was set with her mother's best bowls. When Lettie arrived, bustling inside with the pomp and circumstance of a well-known politician, "I nearly fell," she said. "There's a slick spot just this way coming from the mailbox."

"What were you doing out at the mailbox?"

Lettie hand her a fat envelope. "This was stuck half way between the lid and the box. My guess is someone wanted you to see it from your window. Be careful, is all I can offer."

Curious, Elizabeth opened the letter. She counted four pages with nothing written on them. Then there was the one she looked for. She read, "people are keeping things from you. Your old friend is not A friend and your new friend is dangerous."

Puzzled, she asked, "Lettie, who sends stuff like this? As for old friends, that would be you, Bobby and Elaine. I don't know if Derek would be considered in that group, or not, Catrin would, I guess. But who is my new friend?" Lettie stared at her. "What are you thinking? All I know new would be Joe, and the two that work for Derek, Jeanie and Bill." She laid the letter on the countertop and sit next to Lettie. "Do you think Joe is dangerous? My mother warned me to not go out there."

"I don't know, Doll. Your mother was dangerous." They laughed, as Elizabeth poured the tea.

"Did she change that much after Dad left, or was she always that way?"

"While he was with her she relied on him but when he left there was a rebellious streak. Whoo-ee." Lettie's laughter filled the kitchen. "I tell you she was a wounded warrior. You've heard a woman scorned? Well, there were months of remorse and then came the rebellion, she could do anything, no man could help her they were not her caliber and what she didn't tackle, we did together. Me holding the phone explaining whatever I'd pulled up and she was doing the job." Lettie's laughter was a healing balm.

"She changed then, for the better or worse?"

Lettie considered the question. "Well, it was very tiring and she and even myself, we learned a few things. I believe it was for the better. She wasn't moping around wondering if Frank was coming back."

"What did she find out about Joe that made her think he was dangerous?"

"This chili is good. Aren't you going to eat yours?"

"Good try, but it doesn't work. Yes, I plan to dig in, right now. Maybe you'll tell me later."

Later, before they could dig into really good gossip, Lettie's cell rang. She explained, "The college girls decided to wash clothes and something has happened. They are flooding the basement as we speak, I've been through that mess. You have to open the drain in the floor."

"Do you have to leave?"

"Not if they open that drain. Surely two girls that age can open a drain right by the washer."

The door bell rang. "My goodness," Elizabeth headed to answer. "We are in business, aren't we?"

"Hey, Sis." Thomas James came barreling through the door, lift her up and spun around. "And your friend is right behind me." His eyes were on Lettie standing in the kitchen taking in the excitement.

"Hey, good lookin', how are you?" He had to take Lettie for a little dance around the room. "I got out early and couldn't wait to get here. Nan's on the way, too. Did you know?"

"No, I didn't know." Lettie was beaming. "How are you, Thomas James, or is it Tommy?"

"Come on, Aunt Lettie, you know Nan's going to call me Tommy. Remember when she changed my name?" His eyes went to Derek standing in the living room, "Hey, Derek, come on in here. They got grub. What is it, Auntie, Chili? I'm starving."

Lettie was finding extra bowls. "Good thing I sent the whole pot over. Y'all dig in. Come on in, Honey." She motioned Derek to the table. "Don't' mind her, she's shell shocked. I bet she hasn't had a room full of people since she left the court room, whatta you bet?"

"Hey, Derek, remember that Christmas snow was on the ground and you pulled us behind your gramps truck on that old truck hood we found on the ditch bank?"

"Yeah, I nearly got in trouble for that, your Nan wasn't too keen on it being metal. She said you could have been hurt, or Elizabeth. But she had a hold on you."

Thomas James glanced at Elizabeth. "She's the best sis ever. I wouldn't have any family if Nan and Elizabeth hadn't taken me in." He was devouring the chili. "Eat up, Derek, it's good."

"Why Sweetheart, a good lookin child like you were, someone would have latched on to you."

"Yes, Aunt Lettie, but they're my family and I love them." His words brought a smile to Elizabeth. "Dad brought me here to roam the back woods and they all went right along with me. How old was I, Lizzie?" He slipped into the name his father called her, one he often used himself.

"You were somewhere between three and six when you and Dad came back." Her smile widened. "We learned what fun was when we got you. We couldn't' get our jobs done for following to see what you got into next."

"It was phenomenal, wasn't it, Aunt Lettie. I was the bastard child and Nan loved me like I was her own."

"What a terrible description, Tommy." Everyone laughed. Elizabeth settled down beside him.

"Well, what other woman would take in her husband's illegitimate son?" You know I remember this pretty lady came to the house the day my momma died, she said, who are you? I said Thomas James, they call me T. J. and do you want to work puzzles with me? She said yes, I do and it wasn't long after one day she said, I've had enough of this T.J. stuff. We're going to call you Tommy. I'm named after Dad's father, right, Sis?" Elizabeth nodded. "You all want to play in the snow afterwhile."

"Lord, help us all, Thomas James, your mind just flits here to there. Don't you ever slow up?"

"Can't. Especially here. So much to do, to see. I'm glad Sis is back to stay. Wish I could." He turned to Derek. "How long will you be here? Through Christmas, I hope. We can have the best of times." He elbowed Elizabeth. "I bet you think I made that one up, don't you?"

"No, I know you didn't." She elbowed him back. "Charles Dickens claims that honor. It was the best of times, it was the worst of times, it was the age of wisdom, it was the age of foolishness, it was…." She stopped, wrinkled her nose and said, "I give up."

"It was the epoch of belief, it was the epoch of incredulity, it was the season of light." Thomas James concluded. "The season of light. Birth of Jesus. Families celebrating. Let the good times roll. Right, Derek? So how long will you be staying?"

"I'm considering living here."

"Wow. I envy you. Mosby is one of those little calendar towns, like Currier and Ives and this house is the ultimate to make it believable." He cut his eyes to Elizabeth. "I bet that makes you happy, huh?"

The doorbell rang. Elizabeth welcomed the diversion. Her mother practically fell into her arms. "Elizaabeth, Darling." She reached back taking the hand of the tall gentleman behind her. "Darling, this is my new husband, Jonathan Scott meet Elizabeth, my daughter and in there," she pointed, "is my adopted son, Thomas James, just call him Tommy." She hugged Elizabeth profusely, "Sweetheart, breathe. I know it's not everyday your mother brings home a new husband but we decided it was a good time to be married. And don't worry, no, I haven't been sleeping with Jonathan. He's a Baptist Minister and it isn't allowed."

Thomas James left the table, with an amused laugh. "Sounds like you would have, Nan."

"Shush." She wrapped her arms around his shoulders. "My goodness, Tommy, you've filled out."

"And there is Elizabeth's friend, Derek. Hello, Derek, so good to see you after all these years."

"You, too, Mrs., ah, …"

"Nan, Derek. Let's make it easy. I was hard on you and now that's all behind us. You're on your own." Turning to Johnathan she explained, "I always thought they had such an attraction I was afraid they'd get in trouble and the only way I knew to prevent it happening was to keep them apart." Next she turned to Lettie, "And this, dear Jonathan, is my very dear friend, Lettie, who saw me through thick and thin…stood by me when I was mean as a snake trying to learn how to do things and it was tough."

"She was tough," Lettie agreed. "But not mean, just determined to learn how to care for things." She held out a hand. "Let me take your coat and if you all haven't eaten, there's a huge pot of chili on the stove. Tommy, get more bowls and if you're finished clear your spot for someone to sit there."

"Good thing you kept the big old table, Nancy Ann. I think if Rome could've been built in a day, we would have tackled it right here, don't you?" Everyone settled to eat chili with an occasional remark. Even Elizabeth let her guard down.

"This is nice." She said and her mother's husband met her glance to say, "yes, it really is."

Elizabeth's mind was on a thousand things. First, the fact Derek had returned and her brother not knowing there was a rift had brought him in as though he were family. Then there was the question, did she give back the room to her mother, would she even want that room where she slept with Frank and last what would she feed these people in the morning. That thought brought her back to the table where Jonathan was handing the keys to his car to Thomas James.

"Oh, yes, Darling," Nancy Ann was saying to T.J., "We couldn't come in empty handed when we are appearing out of the dark, uninvited and unexpected, could we?"

"Mother, it's your home. How could you say that?" There was laughter and boos going on.

"Darling, don't let your feathers ruffle, we meant to lighten your load."

"Well, I will be going to work around ten in the morning."

Nancy Ann smiled her eyes on Derek. "It's wonderful you two have reunited and you work for him."

Derek was clearing his throat. "Mild misconception, Mrs…I mean Nancy, Elizabeth doesn't work for me."

"But I thought." Eyebrows raised she waited for an explanation. "I'm sorry, please fill me in."

"I was fired, so I have a different job, now."

"Really, you were fired and you have a new job, and where is that?"

"I told you in our phone conversation, Mother. I work for Joe Belieu at the Club."

Silence hung in the air, as if being digested, until Nancy Ann said, "I thought that was temporary, like one day or something…. Sorry Derek I misunderstood." She held eye contact with her daughter, "I believe I implied you should keep distance from the Club."

"Why is that, Mother? Now's as good a time as any to give me the details. Why?"

"Because we stand by our friends."

"Who are you referring to, Mother? Who are our friends?"

"Catrin." Her mother said through clenched teeth. "I thought you would understand."

"Catrin?" Elizabeth's laugh was full of hurt and anger. "The one person who always, always set out to hurt me and you say that? Thank God Joe doesn't hold those feelings and I might add he's the only one, it appears." She glanced around the room, taking in everyone as Thomas James returned from outside carrying bags of groceries. Elizabeth didn't acknowledge him or them, she was that angry.

"You are supposed to be my family, my friends but you've kept me on the outside, made me feel an intruder that had no one when I wanted to return to Mosby and build a good life. I feel betrayed." She wanted to leave them, find a place she could breathe but there was still no explanation. "Tell me why you stand for Catrin and Joe is off limits, why is that?"

"Ask Joe." Lettie came to her side. "It's not a secret, Lizzie, but not ours to tell. We said we wouldn't. There was so much hurt, when asked to befriend Catrin we all agreed since we live in a small community, if we didn't talk it then no one would know and there would be no gossip."

"I have to get out of here. Mother you are in charge, it's still your house. I'm going for a ride to think and clear my head." She heard the protest and put her hand up. "no, no, I won't do anything rash but I do need to think and for me. I just need space. "I'm glad everyone's here and not to be the party pooper, I'm going to take a little drive and think about what you've said."

She went to the room she had been staying in, removed the personal items she would need later and cleared the dresser top. It was a simple matter, gathering clothes for the next day and what she needed for the night. There was a hush as she retrieved a coat from the rack and slipped out the door to find Derek waiting.

"Come with me, we don't have to talk. I'll drive." Derek reached for her hand as she went down the steps and saw her into the car before sliding in and driving away from the house.

"Why are you doing this?"

"Because I feel your hurt and I decided its time I tell you what happened and that its not a conspiracy, instead I believe for once a group of friends decided to be a friend to someone that was hurting, but in doing so we hurt you. You not knowing was something we didn't think about."

He drove around the main block where the park was handy to the shops for sitting and visiting. "Is it all right with you if we go to my place?" She nodded. "I didn't realize everything was closed." He glanced at the dashboard clock and laughed. "Good reason, I think. Don't you?"

"I admire the view one gets driving by this business. Who designed the building?"

"I did. You may remember how I used to sit and draw as we listened in school. This was an old design I thought would make the most of the scenery behind it."

"Well, it's beautiful."

"Come on, I'll show you the inside where I'm staying."

She took the tour and when they were seated looking out into the wooded area of nothing but trees and grounds that had been cleaned of fallen limbs and debris with only the landscape covered in snow, she said, "tell me what you know."

"We both remember, Catrin always had a wild side and being the daughter of probably the richest man in town she got by with more than the rest of us." Somber eyed, Elizabeth nodded. "I didn't know at the time, maybe you did, Catrin was going to the Club, using fake I D and that's when she met Joe, son of the owners. He was, as I was told, a man at loose ends. Having suffered personal hardship he came to be near his parents. This all happened before we go off to college but we didn't know it. Catrin was pregnant and Mosby being the little Currier and Ives town it's claimed to be, her parents did not want their daughter smeared in any way shape or form. They demanded the Belieu heir marry Catrin, after all they reasoned they were good people, educated and appeared wealthy." His gaze held hers. "If I cut to the long story short version, we can iron out the details later, what it amounts to, if she was to go to College then who would care for the baby? The Collier's decided to adopt out the baby. Joe said no. Catrin was caught in the middle but gave in to her parent's. This was Joe's second upset. He went off the deep end, his parents were afraid he would kill himself or even worse, maybe Catrin.

"Remember, he was trained in combat and survival techniques. Knowing he still loved her, Catrin who by now was living with her parents flaunted herself in front of Joe. This woman who had his child and forged his signature to allow the baby go into adoption procedure, was too much for him to handle. He appeared at the Collier home one night ready to tear the place apart, but for some reason not one of us understands, the Collier's employ guards that wiped the floor with him, laid him up with internal organ damage for over a year. That aged his father along with loss of the baby and he died. It was sad."

"There was a restraining order against Joe," she volunteered. "What else?"

"That's about it. Joe began the search for the child to no avail. Catrin returned to school, angry, disillusioned and ready to go against everything decent because she thought she got a bad deal." He seemed to study the floor before continuing. "You were right. I lied. She would show up at my door, throw herself into my arms and cry for hours. I couldn't turn her away but I never took it farther. I think she loved Joe but her parents threatened to cut her off if she saw him. You know money is important to Catrin." He took a deep breath. "Not making excuses, but she was beat down. Didn't know what to do. Joe, on the other hand said he'd kill her if she let the child go into adoption."

"But now she's taking advantage of your kindness, unless you've changed your mind."

"No, I haven't and I know she took a jab at you that day at the Club."

"That's why you jumped up to berate me, saying I had no right. That's where we began to have trouble." She stood. "Thank you, Derek. Now, if you don't mind, I'd like to go home."

"It's going to be hectic."

"I know," she replied, tiredly. "But they are my people. I want to be with them."

"I fly out to California tomorrow for two days, may I see you when I return, Elizabeth?"

"I don't know, Derek. Let me work on this news a day or two."

The house was quiet when she let herself in. There was a light under the Master Bedroom door. Thomas James was waiting at the top of the stairs. His expression was somber.

"You okay, Sis?"

"Yeah, come on in and let's talk. I want to know how you are."

She lay across the bed and pat for him to join her. "How are you really?"

"You know me, Sis. I'm happy to be with family. What's going on with you? I didn't understand any of what was being said."

"It's just an old friend, T.J., I can't really explain what's happening because it's history."

"But it's not Derek's fault is it? I'd hate to lose him. He loves you. You know that."

"Why do you think that?"

"It's obvious. The way he looks at you. When you were distressed, he was too. I felt it."

She put an arm around his shoulders. "I don't know what we'd do without you."

He leaned over to kiss her cheek. "I think it's the other way around, Sis. I wouldn't have anyone if it wasn't for you and Nan." He rolled over onto his back. "How many people could love their husband's child by another woman? I figure the odds are pretty low."

"They'd have to have a little boy come into their life, like you did ours. A little boy that didn't even have underwear to fit. Can you imagine me and dad shopping for clothes when we had no experience whatsoever? The sales clerk got the picture pretty quick."

"And then Nan finished up, didn't she? Dad told me. I was almost five when he died and he tried to tell me everything."

"What did he tell you about me?"

"He said your sis will always love you. She's got your back."

"That's funny."

"Then why do you have tears in your eyes? You know what else he said?"

"Come on, you were only five."

"He said when the time comes you tell that old boy I said yes, and to treat her right."

"You've never told me that before."

"It wasn't time. Tonight I saw we're getting close."

****

Nan came to check on them. "Jonathan, come up stairs," she called down. "You gotta see this." She waited for him to join her and led him across the hall. "Look in there."

He gave a low chuckle. "Both their feet are hanging off the bed. Aren't you going to wake them?"

"Nah, that would spoil the picture. You got your cell?" She snapped the picture and handed back his phone. "That's worth every mile we traveled. Thank you, Jonathan."

"Honey, if you're happy, as the old saying goes, I am too."

"We're going to have the best Christmas."

****

Elizabeth thought she heard the clock strike. "Eight o'clock? It can't be?" She wiped drool on her sleeve and unwound from the bedspread. Thomas James didn't stir. He was curled in a knot. "Cold, too," she murmured, putting the spread over him. She hurried into the bathroom, shut the door and took a shower. She had forgotten her coat in the newlywed's bedroom. She would wear her mothers.

She was supposed to be at work by ten today and it was nine fifteen. She wanted to talk to Joe. Finding her purse and the black suede shoes she'd placed in the closet downstairs, she left a note and went out into the cold. Today was her first day to switch the uniform for the little black dress. Arriving she retrieved the bag she'd packed from the back seat of the Jeep and went in.

"I knew you'd be baking. The fragrance wafts right out the door and down the street. Either we will have a pack of dogs yowling soon or the neighbors down the road will be coming up the hill."

"Spice cake with coconut-pecan icing," Joe said, smiling, "with or without the coconut and pecans." He turned to look at her, staring a minute before he whistled. "Wow. You look amazing. When you said you would wear your black dress I thought of a pilgrim with a big ole white collar."

She preened. "There's no collar and it ain't pilgrim, pilgrim."

"You look amazing. I said that, didn't I? Well, you do. What's in the bag?"

"Something Nan must have forgotten she had. I'm going to spruce up the table. They're new."

By eleven Joe was dishing food into the warming pans and setting up the buffet. In the center of each white clothed table, one large red poinsettia shined above a crystal vase. The silverware gleamed and the white napkins were curled inside round wood holders. "Looks great, Lisbeth, you make me happy."

"That's nice."

"You seem happier, today. Am I imagining that?"

"Nope. My brother and my mother with her new husband are home for Christmas. They surprised me last night."

"Uh, huh." As ususal he was smiling. "I thought maybe you and the gentleman from California made up."

"Ha. What do you know about anything?" The door opened. "Saved by the bell, Sir." She called back but the stride of her walk faltered when she saw it was Catrin. "Welcome. Are you alone?"

"What does it look like Elizabeth?" She refused her coat being taken and draped it on back of the chair. "Don't you ever let up? Derek was eating out of the palm of my hand until you showed up."

"Really?" Elizabeth was pouring ice water into one of the glasses. "Since you have your hand and don't need a plate, would you like a menu or will you be taking buffet?"

"Actually, I came to talk to you. You must know I won't turn loose of the only available bachelor in

Mosby. You think because you went off and became a lawyer you can scare me off?" Catrin leaned her face against the palm of her hand. "You didn't win the last time, nor will you now. Remember the Soree'?"

Elizabeth gave a low chuckle. "I'm afraid I don't. I saw slutty movement out on the floor and decided any woman was better than that and I left. I heard a certain high society woman made a fool of herself."

"You wouldn't say that if Derek was here. Remember he came to my defense the last time? He will be here soon."

"He must have wings then. He told me he would be in California a few days. I believe he left this morning." Elizabeth laid one hand on the back of a chair. "Oh, poor babe did he forget to tell you?"

Catrin picked up the crystal stemmed glass and threw the water on Elizabeth, just as Joe stepped into sight. "Catrin, NO." She had the silverware in her hand. "Put it down. That could hurt or maim."

"Are you on her side too?" Catrin was near tears. "Always standing up for someone else, huh, Joe?"

"You two know each other?" Elizabeth reached for one of the cloth napkins on the table and begin to blot her face and the front of her dress.

"Do we know each other?" Catrin's laughter was hysteria mixed with sobs. "You idiot, do we know each other Joe?" She had laid the silverware down and reached for the crystal bud vase with the red poinsettia, hurling the vase toward Joe, striking him on the cheek. Before she could move, Joe had crossed in front of Elizabeth, his hand on Catrin's wrist as she searched for the next item on the table. "No, no. You can't touch me, I have legal papers against you…don't you touch me."

"Yes, and you lied about that, didn't you. I didn't touch you but you got your parents to say I abused you. They thought they would run me out of town. Did they know you lied, Catrin? Were you so believable they thought they were doing right in having me thrown into jail and your mother's guards, what did I do to them that they beat me until my insides were bruised? Are you happy, Catrin that I still wear the stripes?"

Joe was screaming. "Tell me, are you happy?" Catrin was crying in earnest now as he leaned over her. His voice was terrible; his eyes smoldering with rage? "You said you were leaving me for another man and you gave our baby into your mother's hands. Who would believe me when the mighty Collier family said I abused their daughter. But who would give their baby into adoption. What kind of mother are you and your own?"

Catrin was crying, sinking to her knees, begging, "Please, Joe, don't hit me." His fist was doubled, she was trembling. "I'm sorry. I've been sorry every day of my life. I can't make decisions, I wait for Derek." Joe grabbed the front of her dress and it ripped. "No, no, it wasn't Derek, he helps me. He loves her, but she doesn't love him. I console him best I can." The dress ripped away, hanging open to the waist, as Joe reached for her hair. "Please, Joe. Please." He was dragging her toward the kitchen. "I'm sorry, I'm sorry. Joe. Joe. Joe, I know where our child is. Mother let me keep her. She's grown, Joe and she's beautiful."

"You lie. You just want me to let you go. This time you are going through the same hell you put me through." The door to the kitchen swung behind them. Catrin's pleading took on a tone of terror and Elizabeth snapped out of the shock of seeing the savagery Joe was putting out. Her fingers fumbled as she picked up Catrin's phone. There was no dial tone. She raced to the kitchen. "You love that beautiful blonde hair, don't you Catrin?" She couldn't believe what she was seeing. "They shaved my head bald, I didn't care but when they stripped me naked and beat me, I began to plan what I'd do to you." Joe ripped his shirt off, his hand still on Catrin's hair. "Look, just look at the damage they did." From the counter he reached for the knife Elizabeth had seen him dice meat. One slice, Catrin's beautiful blonde hair fell to the floor. Her screams were curdling as she slumped thinking he meant to cut her throat but he threw the knife in the sink and pushed her away. "Leave me and never darken this door again. Do you hear me? Get out. I never want to see you again."

"I still love you, Joe." Catrin was taking in the rage, the heavy breathing and his coming back. She scrambled to her feet, gathered the front of her dress and ran out the door, cowering behind the brick wall, thinking he was coming after her. Elizabeth rushed into the dining area, grabbed Cartrin's fur coat and hurried back having to step around Joe, aware of the the deranged look on his face she nearly missed the step as she pushed through the door, slipped on the pavered patio and threw the coat over Catrin's shoulders. "Wait, here. I'll get my car." She fumbled for the keys in her pocket and found them by the time she reached the Jeep. In seconds she was back screaming for Catrin to get in. Catrin moved in slow motion.

Once inside the jeep, she sobbed, "don't take me home. Take me to Derek's."

"He's gone."

"Take me there, I know where the key is. He won't care. I have clothes there." She settled down into the seat, her chopped hair sticking to the back as she tried to curl into a ball against the cold. "I drove him to this. I did it before and I've done it again. You didn't call the police." Her question faded out.

"The phone wouldn't work."

With ten minutes of deep ruts and snow on the side of the road, they were in Derek's drive. It was then Elizabeth noticed Catrin had lost her shoes. Stooping to pick up one of the pavers, Catrin pulled a small plastic bag from beneath, removed a key and unlocked the door. They were inside where Elizabeth had been the night before, while Catrin was removing items of clothing as she walked through the house. She returned with a comb and scissors in her hand. Wrapping a towel around her shoulders, she said, "I want you to straighten up the back of my hair."

"No, I don't cut hair."

"Today, I need you to cut my hair. Right now." She thrust the scissors and comb into Elizabeth's hand. "It can't look any worse. Pick up a lock, estimate three inches and cut until all my hair is that length." She took a deep breath and began holding up strands. "Cut, right there."

An hour later, Catrin came from the bedroom wearing jeans and a sweatshirt that said, Just Try Me. Her hair was dry, gelled and sticking out in spikes, her make up had been refreshed and all in all no one could tell what she had been through. "How does it look to you? My hair?"

"Better than I would have imagined."

Cartrin smiled, "thank you." She sit across from Elizabeth. "I'm going to tell you my side of this story if you promise after I finish you will go check on Joe. He will have calmed down by then."

"Or have killed himself," Elizabeth muttered. "But I will."

Catrin began, "It's true. I did have Joe's baby. I even married him. But Mother had other plans for me. She brought in her idea of what a son in law should be and paid him to court me. Oh, yes, he was very believable as a man who had fallen in love with me. He brought flowers, candy, took me to places Joe wouldn't go but we never made love. I found out later, he had someone back home, in Tennessee.

He was actually related to one of the guards that beat Joe."

She held up both hands to ward off questions. "Let me finish. That's where mother's best laid plans went amuck. He needed money and he didn't care what he had to do to receive the money Mother promised. Joe was jealous." She bowed her head for a minute. "I drove him crazy. I didn't realize until later I loved his caring for me. He would have done physical harm to Gerard, that's the name of the one Mother hired. I stopped Joe in time; that's when the two mother keeps at the house beat him with their belts. You saw the scars. We left him to fend for himself. His elderly parents came home and found him and took care of him with the help of a visiting doctor that determined his insides were bruised and possibly he might have permanent damage. But Joe's body was strong and he bounced back. By the time he could walk again, our baby was removed from this community. It broke his heart. Daddy was able to have the marriage annulled." She stood. "Now, if you will, go back and check on him."

"Just like that, Catrin, you meddle with peoples lives and you don't care what happens to them?"

"Only if it hurts me, Elizabeth. You know that from when we were children. Did you expect me to change?" She gave an evil laugh. "Why do you think my clothes are here at Derek's?"

"All the pleading was an act? I would have sworn you feared for your life."

"Joe loves me, Elizabeth. He won't hurt me."

"You could have fooled me." She let out a big breath of air. "I'm going. Please, the next time you see me, turn around and go the other direction."

"I will if you walk away from Derek. We were meant to be together."

"Do you really think I'm going to let you win this one?

****

Elizabeth considered Catrin's story. She could never believe anything, completely. History was a strange thing, you remembered things you wished you didn't. Joe said Catrin told her parents he abused her, not even seeing his wrath made her believe Joe could hurt Catrin. Abuse, she understood. She had kept that part of her marriage secret. Addison knew how to cut deep, with his acid remarks and then the personal injuries to her body he had studied where to place them so no one would know. She shuddered. She would take that part of her marriage to the grave. Why had she always felt she was responsible for Addison's problem? Now she wondered that she took the blame when she never cast a blow and when it was over he would say, "I'm sorry, Babe, forgive me." And she did.

Chapter 10

She hurried to the Jeep and drove away. Arriving at the Club, she found a dozen or more vehicles in the parking lot. Inside two young women in short black skirts and reveling white blouses appeared to take her to a table.

"I'm Joe's hostess. I had to leave for a bit."

They gave her the once over and replied together, "We're Joe's waitresses. He told us you'd be here.

What do you want us to do?" They pointed toward the kitchen. "Joe's almost got the steaks ready.

Shall we wait for your cue or do what we normally do?"

"Be normal," she replied. "Is he okay?"

They gave her a strange look. "Never better, even forgave our not showing last week."

With a group of arrivals Elizabeth slipped into her new role. They were out of town and had stopped to shop and have dinner before traveling farther. The table where Catrin caused chaos had been stripped clean and reset with the red poinsettia in a different vase. Mentally, Elizabeth was shaking her head that such disruption could disappear as if it never happened.

She was helping clear the out of town group's table when the door opened to boisterous laughter. "Hey, Sis," Thomas James was in the lead, Lettie and her two college girls and Nancy Ann and Jonathan close behind. "We came to check you out."

"We want to say hello to the chef," Nancy Ann added. "Is that possible?" She turned to Lettie, "Don't we?" Elizabeth whispered their request to one of the waitress. "How are you Sweetheart?"

"This is a surprise, Mother." She gave everyone a hug. "I take it no one wanted to cook?"

Jonathan was grinning. "I think we ate all Lettie's chili last night and you have summed it up."

The waitress was handing menus around while Thomas James studied her uniform. "Why aren't you wearing the skirt and blouse, Sis?" Having to answer was cut short as Joe appeared. He gave Elizabeth a wink and went directly to Lettie.

"Hey, you." Joe pecked a kiss on her cheek. "Why haven't you been out to see us?" Not waiting for a reply, he bent to shake Nancy's hand. "I understand congratulations are in order." He offered his hand to Jonathan. "Joe Belieu. Welcome to the Club. Named that because we used to cater mostly to the golfers and such that belonged to the Country Club but as people enjoyed our food we opened to the public and we're glad you are here."

Once more Elizabeth watched as Joe smoothed through a few minutes of welcoming her family and then disappeared to the kitchen leaving them feeling special as if waiting for a treat. In all her years as a lawyer she had used the same tactics on clients, often wondering if it worked. What she had just seen in action certainly worked. She glanced to her mother to find she and Lettie were exchanging a nod. What, she wondered did that mean?

By eight o'clock she was dead on her feet; So much for sleeping cross-ways of a bed. When no one arrived the next thirty minutes, Joe came out to hang the Closed sign on the door and turned out the lights in the dining area. The Waitress's left and she and Joe were alone. She had to know. Going to the outside trash can where none of the left overs had yet been dumped she raised the lid and looked inside. There lay Catrin's hair. She began to laugh. "That was a terrible moment. Scared me to death."

"You are one strange dame." Joe was shaking his head. "But I like your style and thanks for coming back. I was afraid I lost you." He watched her choose an apron to cover the black dress.

"I thought you had gone crazy." She tied the apron strings and began to stack dirty dishes.

"Yeah? I did for a while but it's not worth it. Lately Catrin showing up here after all the years released the beast in me. I wasn't able to fight back the last time. Mrs. Collier's goons horse whipped me but this time I didn't know if they'd show or not and I took matters into my own hands."

"You loved Catrin?"

"Yes, I did. Possibly a part of me still loves her but she took our kid from me." He stopped raking food from a huge pot and gave her full attention. "Did she say another word about our child when the two of you were alone? Do you believe she has our Gracie tucked away somewhere?"

"Your daughter's name was Gracie? No, she only said that she had your baby and also that she married you."

"Madelaine Grace." A sad smile touched his face. "I named her after my Mom because Catrin said she wasn't into names. She would have called her baby."

"Did you try to find the baby?"

"After I was on my feet I did, but that took awhile. I was in bad shape. My Dad died and Mother was at loose ends but I tried. It was believed they let Gracie leave the country with whoever adopted her. This is the first I heard about her being here. I'll start tomorrow checking that information."

"I think Catrin thought you were going to cut her throat."

"At that moment, I could have but I have enough sense to know I don't want to go to prison. They kept me in jail with internal bleeding and broken ribs long enough." He had a way of tilting his head as though looking back. "Lettie knew about it but in an effort to find my little daughter we begged every one that knew to keep the silence, a secret you might say, in order for the search to go forward."

"I understood it was to protect Catrin."

"In doing so, it did."

"I'm surprised it worked, but it did because I didn't know."

"I was upset, to the point I nearly lost my mind. They saw my hurt, even your mother."

"She went through a bit of turmoil herself. My dad and his mistress I guess you'd call her. You met my step brother tonight." She took a deep breath, pausing to look back to that time. "It is a wonder my mother could accept Dad's love child, but she did and I fell in love with a little boy almost three years old who took me into his heart immediately. When he lost his mother it seemed right I help with him."

"And your mother?"

"I thought everyone knew. Dad left her as Thomas James guardian. She loves him and it's mutual."

"That's a blessing."

"You know, Joe, you are a really nice guy."

"Tell you what, Lisbeth," his voice became husky, "if you don't marry that Derek guy, I'm going to ask you to marry me."

"Well I'm honored you would even consider me, but I think you better get to know me, first."

"You're a good dancer."

"Yeah, and you make good chili. But that's not grounds for marriage." They laughed.

She was on her way out the door when Joe called to her. "Elizabeth?" She turned. "Don't take whatever Catrin tells you to heart. She might tell you she's marrying your guy to upset you. She did things like that when we were married. One fellow was hired by her mother but Catrin told me they were head over heels in love and she was going to leave me for him. I was always upset and on guard and you know what? He didn't care a thing about her. He had a girl in Tennessee. Remember, if the fellow was trust worthy when you were young, chances are he still is but Catrin's not."

****

It was nine thirty when she arrived home. Already lights were low, the newlyweds were missing and Thomas James was waiting for her. "That guy likes you. Your boss."

"Well, good evening to you, too."

"Sis, the big tree is missing. Can we put it up?"

"Sure, but not tonight, okay?"

"You've had a busy day?"

"A very interesting day. There's things I have to think over."

"That can only mean one thing. Derek."

"Yeah…maybe part of it. Good night."

"When you get your pajamas on can I come in awhile? I won't talk. I'll just lay there."

Shaking her head, Elizabeth found herself laughing. "Yes, Bubba, you can come in."

****

Catrin's clothing in Derek's home had been a surprise. Catrin knowing where the key was another surprise. Catrin's very confidence that they would marry came as another part of the riddle when Derek had asked her if they could spend time together and try to resurrect their old relationship. She was tired and went to sleep but the dreams came, filled with Catrin's mocking smile and Derek's somber expression as he waited for her decision. "How can I trust you?" She asked as Catrin linked her arm through his. "If I spend one minute with you she has to go. You decide." She awoke. That was the answer.

Oh, no, she forgot Thomas James wanted to come in. She turned over. There he was on the other pillow. He put his finger on the page of the book he was reading and laughed. "Sis, you were cutting logs. You must have really had a hard day."

She punched him. "I did. I'm going to tell you about it, but you cannot tell Mother and worry her."

He listened and when she finished he said, "Sis, if Derek wants the two of you together, you can't let Catrin mess with your mind." He closed the book and lay on his back, his arms behind his head. "She has never been stable, has she?"

"Not really. In the beginning I thought the reason was her parents spoiled her terribly but when she became an adult, wouldn't you think she would see always being self centered no one really likes to be around you?"

"I don't think she wants anyone around except who she chooses, like Derek, or maybe that Joe person. What effect is this having on you? I understand there was a falling our over Catrin years ago, you left Mosby and married but Derek didn't marry. He went off and made a life alone. Do you understand that possibly you were the one in his heart and no one else could replace how he felt?"

"What made you so smart?"

"What would you think if I changed the direction I've been going and enrolled in Seminary. As in, studying to become a minister like Jonathan?" He waited for her reply as she rose up on one elbow staring at him. "I think God placed Jonathan in our midst. When I visit Nan we always have great conversations. I told him I was having second thoughts about going into the business world. He always prays and when he finishes I have this feeling of peace so strong I can't explain it. It's like nothing else I've ever known."

"You'll have to take your time and be sure. I had no idea."

"Neither did I but its growing stronger and I'm going to have to act on it. I don't know what Nan thinks either." He was quiet a moment. "You realize I'd lose the remainder of my scholarships if I do and I'll have to get a job in order to make it."

"Is that why you wanted to come in to my room?"

"Yeah. I wanted to talk to you about it. How do you feel about that?"

"It's up to you, Bub. Where in the world did Mother meet Jonathan?"

"I was with her. We went to church. It was that simple He led in worship."

"Wonders never cease."

"We're all searching for something aren't we, Sis?" His question hit home.

"Yes, we are," she replied.

****

Life went on as usual. A gift shopping spree was in order for Saturday and then on Sunday church with Christmas arriving next week. Derek returned and showed up at the house. At work, Joe was spending every spare minute on the Internet. He must have made a hundred phone calls. Elizabeth wanted to ask but if he needed her he would let her know. Saturday arrived. Elizabeth had coerced the two who were waitresses to cover for her until two o'clock. But she had to be there. Joe had arranged for a five piece ensemble for the event and two large family parties would be going on. As hostess she would help whoever was in charge for each family.

They were standing outside the Bible and Book Store. She was studying the items in the window when Jonathan stepped up to have a look. "Jonathan, would you help me choose a Bible for Jonathan?"

"Has he mentioned needing one, Elizabeth?"

"He told me he had talked to you about what he wants to do next semester. What do you think?"

"He has to follow his heart, Elizabeth. Not me or you could deter him from what's going on in his head. It's a calling and he will be miserable if he doesn't accept it."

"Thank you for taking time to talk and listen to him. He is a good person. He was such a sweet little boy and mother fell for him right off. I think that's what brought her and Dad back together those last years, Thomas James."

"The scripture says a little child shall lead them. Just as it was true Jesus led, your brother did the same."

They went in together while the others watched the parade of whimsical characters march by.

Jonathan found the Bible he thought would be helpful and Elizabeth watched him linger over a book on the disciples. She made a note to return for it on Monday if the time was not right before they left. It would be Johnathan's gift. For her mother she found a silk scarf with all the colors she wore in her clothing. It was going to be a wonderful Christmas. But her heart was torn, what was the appropriate gift to give Derek and should she even think on that avenue; she didn't want to embarrass herself. It was then she ran on to a replica of a vintage map of Mosby with all the shops from their childhood. He could frame it for a picture on the wall. She knew he would love it. For His Grandfather she found a wool scarf, blue the color of his eyes and her heart was happy knowing he would receive it with joy.

She and Jonathan left to join the others when she remembered she had forgotten someone. "I'll catch up," she whispered to Jonathan. "I forgot someone." Joe was deserving of a gift, he had taken her in and made her hostess of his club when he didn't know who she was or where she had been, and that was trust. There was a large glass jar with divided compartments, to drop in change and watch as it rolled through various slides until it came to rest in the right slot. She would put pennies in and on the card write trust. For Lettie and the girls there were gloves and with Jonathan's gift now purchased she was finished.

Leaving the group she arrived at the club to change into a black dress and begin preparation for the Family parties. Joe had hired a young man from the community to help him and Elizabeth could only wonder at Joe's absence. Patty and Sandy were adding greenery to the table tops but it was mentioned something else was needed. She had seen red candles stored in a drawer beside the refrigerator and hurried to get them. This was her first time to see the young man introduced as Martin. She noticed he was skilled with a knife as he diced peppers and one did not miss the muscular build. What was going on here? But there was no time to find or question Joe, it was time to set up buffet. That was when Joe arrived to see how things were going as he gave them all a hug. "Thought I should warn you, Catrin will be in one of the party's," he whispered in her ear.

"Didn't you tell her to not come back?"

He grinned. "You know she can't stay away from me."

"I don't know how you do it. You know she will cause you pain."

"The truth is, Lisbeth, she causes me pain whether I see her or not. She's a scar on my heart."

"You still love her?" He nodded. "Oh," she groaned, "I thought you were a sensible man. Just don't kill each other." His laughter spilled out but she wasn't feeling it.

"Remember, a five string ensemble will arrive any time to set up in the North corner. Be sure no one moves tables in that area, in case someone wants to dance. It seems always at Christmas a few become nostalgic and we see them on the floor."

"Really?" She waited for him to elaborate but he turned and was gone.

They were in to the second hour when Catrin's party arrived, couples, except for Catrin. Elizabeth was relieved to see Derek was not part of the group. It was after the meal was served the ensemble began to play waltz music and the couples took to the floor. Just as she was wondering what Catrin would do, Joe in full dress tuxedo came from the back and offered her his hand. The guests at other tables were awestruck as the two danced across the floor. Catrin was magnificent in red organza, Joe handsome in the black tux. Elizabeth stepped back to watch. There was such peace on their faces as they danced, each step in synch. They were in perfect form. Surely at one time there was no turmoil. Her heart was full as she watched. Why was there ugliness in the world when there could be beauty?

The dance finished, Joe bowed to Catrin and returned with her to the table. There were introductions and hand shakes and then again Joe discreetly disappeared. There was a rise of mystery in the room, perhaps people were aware of the altercation of the previous week. Whatever the mindset Catrin reigned but she avoided eye contact with Elizabeth who was amazed that Joe was able to direct the function of the kitchen and still seem to remain cool and calm as twice more he returned to dance with Catrin.

Stilll, Elizabeth was relieved when the night's work was over and there were no casualties.

At home she found Thomas James and Derek waiting for her. She knew immediately her brother had a question. "Aren't you two the budding buddies?" Derek grinned. "What do you want, Thomas James?"

"Can we decorate the big tree now?" He reminded her of when he was twelve year old.

"May I have a moment to change into something appropriate?"

"I don't know," Derek offered, "I kind of like you in that black dress."

"You will like me even better in my old black joggers."

"How was it at the club?"

"A fun packed hour of suspense and mystery."

"You guys are such spoil sports. I saw another box of ornaments. I'm going down to get them."

Once they heard Thomas James on the basement stairs, Derek began to question Elizabeth.

"Catrin was there, huh?" He was shaking his head. "I don't doubt it, but no murder. Right?" He took her hand and pulled her close. "I'm going crazy here, Lizzie, wondering if you intend to let me back into your life. I've waited for you, all these years, does that count for anything?" For a moment he appeared to have a sad thought. "Tell me now if you cannot accept us being together. I will be disappointed but I'll have to live with that. I want to marry you. Please… think about the years we've missed. Tell me what you want."

Thomas James came to the door, "Guys. The tree. She is a waiting….just like me. Come on."

******

By the time the clock chimed ten, the tree was completely decorated. "Now, it matches the rest of the house," James Thomas agreed.

"I thought we'd never get to it. This is one of my first memories. I have thought about it a lot. Few women would take in their husband's child like Nan did." He grinned, reaching over to hug Elizabeth, "But God gave me a sis to love and to love me." He put a big kiss on her cheek. "Thanks, Sis."

Derek was taking it all in. When Thomas James loaded up boxes to take to the basement, he pulled her over to the sofa. "Sit, you are dead on your feet." She settled back as he sit on the edge facing her, "Have you thought any more about us picking up where we left off some eighteen plus years?"

"Yeah, I have, but I'm not sure you will want to hear it." She yawned, as his arm went around her.

"Try me."

"When I took Catrin to your house last week, I found it interesting she had clothing there, but more than that she not only knew where the key was, she felt completely at home, down to having personal items there and she did tell me the two of you are getting married." Yawning again, she finished, "I can't go back to Catrin's antics after all these years and I am not interested at all if you have mentioned marriage to Catrin. She's made those awful insinuations that you fathered her child but Joe says he can claim that one, a hundred percent." She wrapped an afghan around her shoulders. "I'm cold."

He gave her a dubious look. "Who knows what Catrin will tell. She did check on the house before I moved back, about her clothing I don't know, about marriage I have never once entertained the thought. Catrin is a loose canon. I can't figure out that family. Never could."

"Why do you think they have only male servants?"

He shrugged, "Stronger physically. I don't know why they need them but as I understand they've always had them. Catrin's parents are an oddity and they make me uncomfortable." He settled in to hold her hand. "Either give me an answer tonight, about us, or I will not bother you again. I can't go on like this. It's not like me to lose control of myself but I've waited all these years, things keep happening and I need to know where I stand. Do you understand what I'm saying?"

She nodded. "You sound like a business man. Maybe I sound a little strange to in what I said, but I think we are both at a cross roads. I think of you and the history we had together before I left Mosby. Do people really find each other again and have these conversations?"

"Well, we are. You married. Tell me, was it worth it, considering the divorce?" He studied the tree they'd just decorated. "I always remembered how your mother decorated. I guess I had that wistfulness Thomas James had, too. I wonder if he didn't have a more rounded childhood than I did."

He took a deep breath. "So here we are, tell me before I leave…I truly mean it, I can't go on wondering if you consider marrying me or not and then one day you say, don't come back, so it's tonight or never."

"I wish you wouldn't put a time limit on something so important."

"Elizabeth, you know. I know you do, because of how I feel. What is time when there's a second chance? Do you grab it and start living life, or go slow and maybe something happens and you have regrets."

She yawned behind her hand. "It's not that." She leaned forward, trying to clear her head of the tiredness she was experiencing. "It's just been an extra busy day and you've caught me off-guard."

"Is it Joe? You don't understand I get so lonely for you, I'm afraid I'll ask someone else…"

She laughed. "Why would you say that? You know you would never do that. Anyway, it's not Joe."

"I overheard a couple were dancing at the club. I thought it was you and Joe. They said it was…"

"It was awesome," she interrupted. "It was Joe and Catrin. He still loves her, after all the problems."

"She almost killed him, two ways, I heard, getting rid of the baby, and divorcing him. I don't know him that well. Until you went to work there, I steered clear of the club. Now I'm a bit jealous of him, because of you. So, what do you have to tell me?" He assumed she was quiet, thinking.

Head on the back of the sofa, cover pulled up to her neck, Elizabeth was sound asleep.

Her brother came bounding up the stairs. Derek was straightening Elizabeth's sleeping body on the sofa, and covering her with the afghan. "What do I do now? She is so tired I hate to wake her and I'm guessing she will go to work again tomorrow?"

Thomas James tilt his head, looking down on his sister. "I'll check on her before I go to bed." He nodded toward the stairs, "considering you'd have to carry her up those stairs, I'd hate to have to do that, so I certainly won't encourage you to."

"She's not heavy."

"No, but there's a lot of stairs and you don't want broken bones if you drop her." He grinned. "She's safe in my hands. Let me tell you what I remember that first Christmas Dad brought me to Safe Haven."

He glanced at the clock on the wall. "You got anywhere to go?"

"I have the rest of the night, what's left of it." He followed Thomas James to the matching chairs across the room. There they sit in the glow of the Christmas tree. "I was waiting for an answer."

"You remember how it was Derek, I was too young to understand the whole thing. My mother was gone, my Dad was doing his best, I remember Elizabeth was with us a lot and I was little but

I kept hearing the two say, Mom won't like this, or your mother wouldn't understand and I didn't know who they were talking about but I didn't like her. While on the contrary I loved Nan, I just didn't know she was the same person as Mom."

"So then I hear Dad on the phone asking Nan if we can come for Christmas and I was ecstatic, one happy little boy. There may have been a lull between Nan and Dad but she had this house decorated one end to the other, my room was what any little boy would want. She had come up with one of those horses that had stirrups, and made the sound of a horse running when I got on it. There was a cowboy hat, toy guns in a holster. That's not allowed now, and furry things you put on your legs."

"Chaps." Derek couldn't take his eyes off Elizabeth. Had she even heard what he said?

"Yeah. The room had a small tree and it wasn't decorated but every day for that week before Christmas we went out for a walk, Nan, Dad and me and we looked for things like pine cones and gum balls off gum trees and pretty rocks, now that was hard to find with snow on the ground and did I say she had these cowboy boots that fit perfectly that she'd tie plastic bags around so I wouldn't ruin them or my feet get wet and I could wear them on those walks. Those pine cones and rocks and gumballs we brought home and cleaned up and we'd go upstairs and trim my tree." There were tears in his eyes.

"How could you not love a Nan like that? You know what happened? I think Dad fell back in love with her or maybe he never quit loving her and what happened between him and my mother was just a fender bender in the jist of things and," he grinned, "They all just happened to get me in the process."

"Where are they now, Nan and her new husband?"

"They retire early. He's writing a book. You know he's a minister and Nan, takes a nap." He laughed. "Did you think they'd left or we were hiding them away? Their car is in the garage."

"No, it was my understanding they came to stay for Christmas." He sound a bit wistful. "I actually considered asking Elizabeth to marry me but thought maybe it was too soon but I did wonder if she'd marry me while they're here." He let out a breath of pent up air. "I wanted an answer, tonight."

"Whoa. That's pretty quick considering all that's involved."

"Why? I love her. What's the big issue? Besides my dancing with Catrin eighteen years ago?"

Thomas James whistled. "Friend, if you don't know, I think you need to have a little talk with your woman. I don't have a girlfriend and don't want one until I finish what I'm getting ready to do with my life but I can tell you from this family's history, you can't have two women. You know Catrin means to own people and no doubt she would make your and Elizabeth's life a living hell, no cursing intended. You will never gain Elizabeth if you don't make it plain to Catrin she has no rights, nothing but friendship, void of private meetings, personal calls and the like of which she would do."

"You think? Elizabeth's words were I won't go back to Catrin's antics and if you've offered marriage to her, we are through. So you think she means it?"

"Yeah, I do and it sounds like you have."

"I'll admit a cold sweat broke out on my brow when she began but no, I haven't. Never." He stood. "I think I better leave on that one, it kind of puts the starch in me. She deserves the world and I want to give it to her but she said Catrin has moved clothes and personal items into my house while I was gone. I have this sneaking feeling she might be there waiting for me and I've got a job to do."

He bent to kiss Elizabeth's cheek. "I won't let this happen again. I've waited all these years. I'll let myself out."

After a minute's consideration, being a brother Thomas James decided what he must do.

"Sis. Sis." Thomas James was holding her hands pulling up. "Come on, let me help you up the stairs.

It's past midnight." He pulled her feet off the sofa, "Come on, Sis, let's get up those stairs. Okay?"

He set her alarm for nine, pulled a second cover over the afghan and went to his room. She was going to wonder why next morning she was laying cross ways on the bed again and still in her jogging suit. He had to laugh. These people he loved fit right into the category of those he was reading about in the Bible. If he was going to be a shepherd, he better ace the material. There was peace in his soul, he'd made the right decision because Jonathan said if there's peace you've done right, if there's upset or chaos you better rethink the matter, you're probably wrong. He sighed, all is well. He still hadn't told Nan.

****

Catrin listened for sound coming from Derek's room. He had tried to make her go home but she outlasted him. "You can sleep on the couch," he said, "but don't you dare come near my room."

She gave a silent wicked laugh. He was so afraid she would mess up his relationship with Elizabeth. Why, she had been doing that thirty years now, hadn't she? She didn't know why. Elizabeth was a nice enough person; once they'd been friends but Derek got in the way, they both liked him. The problem was, Derek liked, no strike that out, Derek loved Elizabeth. Who loves me, she wondered and she knew and she loved him too, but she and Joe had this passion about too many things and they might end up killing each other. Daddy had their marriage annulled. He said it was Mother's idea, not his. Why did he bend and bow to her? Sybil, her mother was one selfish bitch. I know, I know, she whispered in case God was listening and He probably was. Sometimes she felt him, like a prick a rose bush makes to one's finger, other times she cast a blind eye because she didn't want to see him or think he saw her. She was one to do her own thing, let the pieces fall where they might and hurt whoever as long as it wasn't her. Right now, she was sending a message. That ought to bring Elizabeth down the lane. Catrin laughed, silently, of course, she was on dangerous ground of losing Derek's friendship and she'd never been without that. There, the text went out under anonymous. Only a genius could track her. Joe was a genius. For a minute a pang of regret hit her heart and a tear slipped down her cheek. Where was mother keeping their child? If ever she had a second chance to be a mother was she strong enough for the task? How did one put aside selfish desires for the good of someone else? She slipped back to the sofa, pulled the cover to her chin and went to sleep. That would never happen, seeing her child again.

****

Elizabeth awoke with a bitter taste and dry mouth. She searched for her cell to use the light going down the stairs. She fumbled and caught the wrong button. Messages came on and one caught her attention. She read the text, *take it from one who has been there. Are you interested in knowing your man is entertaining Catrin Collier? Are you interested?* What? Who? How would anyone know she was…wait a minute just because Derek's car had been there a lot recently didn't mean anyone in Mosby made connections, did it? Or could they mean, no, surely, not Joe.

Taking a bottle of water from the frig, she checked the time. Nearly two o'clock? She had taken a nap and she didn't even remember going up stairs. She had to get hold of herself. The Club hours were killers. True she went to work late for many workers but on the feet was gruesome, but then wasn't that how she made a living before, late hours studying cases, on her feet in the court room. What was different? Well, lately the drama and now this. She read the text again. Then it hit her, Derek said he wanted an answer before he left. He was adamant she knew what she wanted. Yes. She knew.

Her coat was hanging on the rack by the door and her keys were in the pocket. She capped the bottle and left it sitting on the table. She wouldn't be gone long. It was time to see if Derek was the man he said he was. If he was, she had the answer. She locked the door and got in her car.

For weeks now, someone had been checking on Safe Haven or someone that was staying there. They had all made a remark about someone casing the joint. But this was real, now she assumed it was the one who sent the text. Who would know her phone number? But you can get anyone's information on the net, she reasoned coming to the four way stop. Straight ahead was Derek's headquarters and home.

Was she out of her mind? Questions kept coming, all with the intention of undermining her quest. She pulled in the lane and advanced toward Derek's quarters. There it was as bright as day under the security light of the business which was a stone's throw away from the small home, Catrin's car. It was dark inside the house, not one light. Angry, she backed out of the lane, her hand on the horn. Glancing up she saw a light come on and a woman's form at the open blind window and then a man stood behind her. She reached the end of the lane, turned the lights off knowing they could not recognize the make of the car causing the commotion and when she was a hundred feet down the street turned them back on. Neither one had a right to know her shame, believing Derek and praying she could trust him. She drove home the tears she had stored up for months wet on her cheeks. She crept inside like a thief out of the night and up the stairs before anyone knew she had left. Tomorrow was another day. She had to get this out of her system; this was not the answer she envisioned.

****

Nancy slipped quietly out of the bed, not wanting to disturb Jonathan. She heard crying. First she listened thinking it was a dream, but the sound came again. From upstairs. It was Elizabeth. She went up, listening again. It was as she thought Elizabeth's room and she went in. Even Jonathan mentioned the turmoil Elizabeth was trying to handle by herself. She had experienced so much alone; but this trying to decide if she and Derek could build trust of each other again and with Catrin always in the picture doing what she did best, it was no easy decision. Catrin was always a problem but that was the least of her worries right now as she bent down to study her daughter's face. Wet with tears. She sit on the side of the bed. "Elizabeth, darling, wake up. Let me help you." But her daughter didn't stir. It was a low pitiful sound that accompanied her tears; grieving in her own way. She felt if she could waken her, Elizabeth would be fine. But her daughter was in deep sleep. After several tries Nancy Ann slipped out of the room and back to bed. Jonathan pulled her close. "Don't worry," he whispered, "She will be all right. It is a big decision and she needs time. She has been through a lot, she's just cautious."

"What if she misses an opportunity to have a happy marriage the second time?" She smiled in the dark. "Like me." She took a deep breath, patted his arm and turned to face him. "I had no idea God would give me a second chance, with you." He kissed her.

"I will never forget those lonely hours after Em died, seven must be a blessed number because that's how many years it took until a certain single lady was sitting in the congregation. God put her there just for me. I'm forever grateful." He hugged her tight to his chest. "Why weren't you there quicker?"

"It took me that long to realize I could afford it and that it was no one's business if I traveled." She sighed. "You're sure my daughter will be all right?"

"Faith, love, faith and trust. Remember we have to believe God has a plan for us."

****

Thomas James heard the sobbing. Alarmed he sit up in bed. The sound came from Llizzie's room.

He had to wonder what was the depth of the problem she was crying over. It seemed things were going to be better for her and Derek. Maybe she was just tired. The Club was pushing the hours and she was staying with the job. Funny, she would accept being a hostess for a club, but Lizzie for all the quiet person she was liked people and wanted to help them. He knocked on the door, she didn't answer and it was not completely shut; he went in. "Liz? What's wrong?" But she wasn't awake. He glanced at the clock. Seven. He stooped down by the bed. "Liz. Wake up. Come on, you've gotta come outta the cry-ing." She stirred, pened her eyes and looked cranky.

"Good morning."

"That's debatable. What are you doing in here waking me?"

"I was worried."

"Worried?" She yawned and stretched. "Why are you worried?"

"You were crying."

"I was not." Indignant, she swung her legs over the side of the bed and sit there. "I'd know."

"Well, you may know but this time you don't know." He moved her over and sit beside her. "So, what is bothering you? It has to be something, Lizzie, people don't just cry in their sleep for nothing."

"What are you all of a sudden, a shrink?"

"Nah, just your little brother concerned over you crying. If it's over that guy at work, don't.

"Honestly, he's the least of my worries. If I was crying, which I doubt, it was probably over Derek acting like he cares and yet every time he pleads his undying love he is with Catrin."

"I am completely in the dark what you are talking about. Last night he indicated to me he was going to find her and make things understood that he loves you and plans to marry you."

Tears of disappointment welled up in her eyes. "Then why was she there last night?"

"How do you know this, Lizzie?"

"I know because when I woke I drove by last night and her car was there. The house was dark but when I honked the horn immediately the lights came on and first it was Catrin at the window and next he stood behind her. If I were a lawyer, I'd say that's pretty damming evidence."

"I feel really bad about this. I know he wanted you all to marry while Nan and Jonathan are here."

"What a pitiful way of showing it."

"Maybe he couldn't get rid of her."

"I don't know, I feel like someone pumped the air out of me and I have to go to work."

"Want me to go with you?"

"What would you do?"

"I don't know but I know I'd enjoy trying about anything."

"Go get on a pair of khakis and grab your sport coat, we'll see, or you can come around four."

"Four it is." He grinned. "I don't want to peel potatoes."

"We don't peel, we bake to go with the steak. Remember that and va-moose, I gotta get ready."

****

Chapter 11

She cleared the drive to find Joe running alongside the Jeep. In one hand he had a brief case. She rolled down the window. "Are you waiting for me?"

"I am. I have something to tell you."

She put the car in park and looked upward, "Please, God, let him tell me he asked Catrin to marry him and she said yes."

"I'm strong but not that strong," he quipped, "Besides, I've asked and she always says no."

"The things I'm learning about you. So what's so important you meet me at my car."

"You are a licensed attorney at law, Right?"

"Yes. This state, now. What about it?" Suddenly it dawned on her. "Catrin's alive, isn't she?"

"Yes. I haven't seen her. But," A smile flashed on his face. "This is the best. I think I've found my daughter. IF I have, I need to know the next steps to getting custody of her."

"You mean she doesn't live around here?" He got in and opened the brief case.

"No, she doesn't. I think it's Catrin's mother's way of keeping Catrin from wanting to see her."

"Where is she?" She wasn't expecting to hear the name of a girl's boarding school on the East Coast.

He handed over two pages of information. "I don't get it." She was scanning the pages. "For one thing, your custody was never repealed, two, the distance and how did you get this info?"

"I have friends in high places. You are one of them." He grinned. "I am so happy. Can you get the ball rolling for me. I'll have to find someone to cover for you this evening, of course."

"Suffice to say, I can take care of that, if you agree. My brother is dropping in around four. How about he does the hosting tonight? I'll clue him in and I'll bet you he is a natural at it."

Joe kissed her cheek. "Whatever you say, Counselor. Wonders never cease in you, do they?"

"If you only knew." She was already on it, her head was filling up with past cases. "We should try to accomplish this by Christmas Eve then you both will have a great Christmas. Will she remember you at all?"

"I don't know. That troubles me. I fought to see her until she was five and then she disappeared."

"It's a matter of fact you are on record as her father. Now, if I can call in a favor from my dad's old friend. You need to purchase a ticket to fly her home. With the right papers I think that can be done."

"Use my office in the house, Lisbeth. I assume I met your brother the other night?"

"Yeah, the young handsome one, resembles George Clooney, just like my Dad." They laughed.

****

"There was never a more perfect ending to a day," she quipped when the club closed at nine that night and Joe accompanied Thomas James into his office. "So how was hosting, Brother?"

"There's more to it than I thought, but Patty and what's her name were very helpful. They even invited me to a party tonight but I said I was already tied up." She was puzzled. "With you."

"Okay, Joe, we're outta here. If I were you, I wouldn't say anything about the arrival until the Big package is here."

"Sounds good to me. I'm going to clean house, tonight for my special guest. See you tomorrow."

"What's in the big package?" Thomas James asked before getting into his vehicle.

"A big surprise," she replied, "a very good surprise." She thought a minute. "Could you pick up a gift tomorrow, something a late teen would like. I think she's seventeen or eighteen." She saw his curiosity. "It's for a possible dinner guest Christmas Day. Mother is planning the dinner, isn't she?"

"How did you guess? I saw the list on the table this morning. It will be a Nan feast."

****

As if in answer to the question, arriving at Safe Haven, the doors to the formal dining room were open, the table was dressed in a sparkling white table cloth, with a Christmas runner the length and red candles placed in the center. Two extra tables had been set up, wearing identical dress. The chandelier had been dusted and gleamed blessing over the grandeur of her mother's favorite china, stemware and silverware.

"Hmmm, the trappings," she said and Thomas James nodded.

"This is what I remember," he said. "It makes me so happy. I hope I find a girl to love just like Nan."

Elizabeth was laughing when Nancy Ann followed by Jonathan came bustling into the room. Both were wearing white chef hats and aprons. Elizabeth and Thomas James exchanged looks.

"What? We're just being professionals. It never hurt anyone to play a game and have a bit of fun.

We counted and we believe we can seat up to thirty people in this room. I'm so glad my grandparents looked ahead when they planned this house."

Thomas James replied, "It's a grand old house. I'm glad Elizabeth hasn't thrown us out, yet."

She elbowed him. "It's Mother's house, goose."

Nan looked from one to the other and then to Jonathan. "My silly children. I split it with Elizabeth.

When she pays me half, its hers. Sorry, Tommy, all you get is the car and your education."

"Which will cost you more than the house, right?"

"Your scholarships help."

Now Elizabeth and Thomas James exchanged worried looks. "I'm going up to change," she said.

She had barely cleared the room when Nancy pulled Tommy into the kitchen. "What is going on with your sister? I heard her crying last night. I checked on her but she was sound asleep." Nancy took a deep breath, as though what she remembered was painful. "I feel quite worried."

"Tell me what you're thinking." Tommy waited. "Go on, I might can help."

"Well, she did that after her father, your father died. Once she was in deep sleep, I would hear her moaning and the sobbing would go on for a while. It was like listening to someone grieving, and I think that's what it is now, a deep loss, but she's happy over Derek now, so that can't be it."

"Not necessarily. Derek was here the other night and said he had plans for them. Marriage. When he left Sis was in deep sleep, then she woke up and without my knowing drove down to see him and guess what? She had told him the only way they could have a future was to get rid of Catrin's influence."

"She's right," Nancy agreed.

"Except for all his good intentions, there it was past midnight and Catrin was at his home."

"Oh, no, so she has called it quits? I hate that, she's always loved Derek. No wonder she's hurting."

"Does it ever enter your mind, for all you've done, we are still a dysfunctional family?" He grinned, laying an arm around her shoulder. "You are exceptional but you can't make us normal, we are who we are."

"In other words, It is what it is. This time she thought things would work out. She does a good job covering the hurt, but then there's the sobbing. Let's think on this; right now, I've got to get in the kitchen, Jonathan's trying to make pie crust."

"That may be dysfunctional, too, for a minister. We'll have to watch him, he may fit right in." She was going. "By the way, love may not die but this romance is in deep trouble."

****

It was the night before Christmas eve. They were in the family room, Jonathan had opened a game to play when the doorbell rang. It was Derek. "I really need to talk to her," he said. Thomas James shrugged. "She misunderstood. It's my fault just like the last time."

"She's a big girl, I don't know what to say but I'm certainly not her boss." He motioned up the stairs. "She went up to get a tablet so we can keep score. You can play, if you promise not to win every time."

"First things first, I have to talk to her. I tried to make Catrin leave that night but she would not go home to her mother. What could I do? She slept on the sofa and I locked my door, because you never know what Catrin will do. She defies most women's stubbornness. She drives me nuts when she's like that. Deliberately, I suspect."

"Good luck then, if there was anything any one of us could say to change her mind, we would."

Thomas James watched Derek go upstairs. He shook his head. I need to pray about this, he was thinking. Silently, he turned aside. "Lord, you said we could go into our closet to pray and it looks like we're going to need to do that with Elizabeth holed up in her room, Derek trying to make amends and Lord, you alone know what Catrin is doing, or has planned. Since I'm new at this, I'll ask you to forgive my own transgressions and then consider I'm learning to talk to you in a new way. I think use to I just ask for things but now I remember Nan telling me it's wise to thank you first before I begin all that selfish stuff. So, I'm asking forgiveness and I'm thanking you for the only family I have and asking your favor on each one. I'll learn how to pray as time goes on but I really do like just talking to you. I'll leave it at that because I know you've got this. Your eye is on each one of us. Thank you for that and right now, help Derek to understand he needs to find you again, if he's lost you. Amen"

****

Elizabeth stepped out onto the upstairs landing but hearing that familiar voice, she stepped quickly back out of view and into her room. She could not face Derek. They had planned a beautiful day together, this Christmas, and then he had gone back on his word. Now he would expect her to forgive and forget. How could she? Sinking onto the bed, she shook her head wondering how long he would wait. She simply could not face him. She was never one to cry, but this time the hurt had intensified due to her own foolishness in believing they were finally able to communicate without Catrin standing between them. Now she must accept there was nothing to that. She was tired of fighting Catrin. She turned off the light, locked the door and got into bed. When she heard the light tapping she ignored it.

She had nothing to say to him.

****

She needed time away from her family. They knew Derek had been there last night and she would not talk to him. She didn't need their advice. She dressed, found a black dress to slip into at the club and left. If she had to drive around all day, anything was better than the questions they would ask. Glancing at her hands on the steering wheel, she was disgusted her nails were in such a state of neglect. She wheeled into Macy's Salon and went in.

"Oh, Honey," Macy crooned, "you need your hair styled. Oh, you want your nails done, too?" She was stepping around like a mother hen. "Honey, I don't believe I know you and I've been here five years."

"No, I'm new in town."

"I thought so, now you just lean back. I'll shampoo and while we condition, I'll have Darla start on your nails." She called to the back and Darla, a plump little darling of teenhood came out. "Don't you worry none, now, Honey. My Darla knows how to do nails but your hair needs conditioning. This is Christmas Eve and I know a knock-out like you has plans." She leaned down. "You do, don't you?"

She was shampoo'ed, conditioned, curled, then straightened and all the while Darla sat chewing her gum patiently waiting. By the time Elizabeth sit at the nail table, Macy's other clients had arrived, among them Catrin Collier. She ignored Elizabeth but to Macy and everyone else she went around showing the new diamond on her left hand ring finger. Elizabeth was curious, as to a name but none was mentioned. She wouldn't know the person anyway and good luck to him.

It was as she paid, ready to leave, she heard Catrin's raucous laughter. "it was so unexpected," she was saying. "For years we've spired and then last night out of the blue…it was like the answer to a prayer, sweet and caring…Derek…" Elizabeth handed Darla a twenty and hurried out the door, and once in the car put her sunglasses on and drove away. She thought she would be crying. The sunglasses would conceal her misery but she didn't cry. She couldn't even think. She was that numb. She drove out of town, leaving the small rural community of Mosby behind.

****

She hadn't been out of town in the time since she had returned to Mosby. All she could think at this moment was what had seemed a nice dream and a blessed life had disappeared. Now that it was over she could admit to herself, she had come home to find peace from a troubled marriage that had never been stable. Addison should never have married, and probably his only reason was to be cared for. In the department of personal maintenance, Addison needed someone to take care of him all the while wandering from one affair to another and never understanding the hurt piled on his wife.

How many times had she questioned her own fault in the situation and tried yet another approach to make their marriage work but Addison only took for granted what she gave and went his happy wandering way until the day she said she could no longer excuse what he was doing because she was tired of people talking behind their backs originally and now openly. That was the last straw. He agreed and the filing for divorce was not contested.

Safe Haven must have been a figment of her imagination. Look what happened. On and on she drove, coming into the city and seeing a small park she entered and found a spot to stop, to get out and walk as she tried to understand the emotions she was suffering. Yes, she was tired last night and yes, Derek gave her an ultimatum. "Tell me tonight, Elizabeth, I can't go on like this. Sometimes I fear I'll ask the first person I meet to marry me, I am lonely and I've waited all these years for you but you seem uninterested in sharing life with me." She could hear his voice in her head, but she had been so tired she had perhaps lost the true arrangement of words, but never the meaning and she had not replied. No, she had gone to sleep to awaken hours later and drive to his home, perhaps to tell him yes, and found Catrin there. Now, today. Her heart cried out, her mind screamed, how could I have done this?

A small glen of trees and age old rocks tall enough to sit on came into view. Something about the spot seemed familiar as she settled onto one and looked around. Concealed by a second row of trees, she saw the school where Mosby had bussed students years past when the roof was blown off their school during a tornado. So this was where Derek had led her that day when she heard her father's voice and saw him with a woman and a small boy. Catrin claimed the boy was her father's son, but her father said Sarah had a child when he met her. The boy died. Thomas James, named after his father was his and Sarah's only child.

Derek first ask her to marry him when they were Graduates preparing for college. "Wait for me, Elizabeth," he said, "four years and then a lifetime, eternity, together." Left behind by his mother and his father, Derek had a fear she would say no, but she waited while Catrin managed to attend college at the same school as Derek.

All that happened in the eighteen years between leaving Mosby and returning filed through her mind. She was at a loss. She had failed. Again. She believed in God, attended church, but still she failed. Quietly, alone, she let her mind settle to the prayers of childhood when she truly believed and then her father left. She married Addison and they parted. Was this to be her lot in life?

"Lord", she prayed. "I need you to still the anxiety of my heart, to deal with the situations around me. Help me to love others and be able to forgive, not just those who hurt me but myself where I make bad decisions." She took a deep breath. "Thank you for Mother and T.J. coming home for Christmas. Help us to have good days together before we part and Lord, guide me and don't give up on me in the days ahead. I need you and I'll try to listen. Now I've got to go back to Mosby and go to work. It's Christmas Eve, Lord. It's almost your Son's birthday. Help us all to keep that in mind as we are together. I can't do this alone but maybe I can do my best with your help." Amen.

****

For all the turmoil she experienced leaving Mosby, for now a peace settled into her heart. She returned the same route she had used to arrive at the park and drove to the Club in time to help the girls prepare for a number of reservations and those who would stop as they traveled by Mosby. Slipping into the black dress and high heels, a glance in the mirror approved the new hair style and she was impressed as if she were looking at someone else. Smile, the mirror seemed to say and she tried.

Joe whistled when he saw her. "When I slip into the tuxedo, you will have to dance with me, tonight." Smiling, he ask, "is that all right with you?"

Noting the smile, she said, "You seem mighty happy. Need to share anything?"

"My girls coming home," he replied, "and your mother sent an invitation for dinner tomorrow. Did you know about that?" She nodded. "She even said bring whoever I wanted. How nice is that?"

"I guess you'll find out when you meet our dysfunctional family."

"I'll fit right in," he replied, stooping to plant a kiss on her cheek. "Have I said thank you, lately?"

****

"I forgot to tell you," Joe said as he passed by carrying a huge glass bowl filled with ambrosia, to place on the buffet. "The ensemble will be arriving, be sure to set them up in the regular place and keep the dance floor cleared of extra tables. It's going to be festive, Lisbeth."

"Then you better get into your duds," she quipped as the clock chimed and the first party arrived for seating. He grinned and hurried to the back. He seemed pretty chipper. She assumed the daughter was on her way. That would make a father glad. The Club was lit by a thousand little twinkling lights and even the sadness of her heart allowed happiness to share with those she served tonight.

Still, she waited, and it didn't happen, Catrin nor Derek came and she was unsure whether she was happy or sad over that situation but when she danced with Joe she caught his newfound spirit of hope refreshing. "You are keeping something from me," she whispered as they danced. He bent low to say, "You will find out soon enough. I don't keep secrets from my attorney but sometimes a nice surprise is the only gift I can give her." She thought on this. "Me?" She asked. He nodded. "Yes, You."

The evening came to a close. Elizabeth headed home, too tired to think further. Showering, slipping into pajamas and into bed was the last thing she remembered until waking Christmas morning.

"It's nine o'clock. Get up." Thomas James fell on thebed, making it bounce off the floor.

"Get out. I'm sleeping."

"You are not. I saw your eyes open. Let's go see if there's gifts under the tree for us, from Nan."

"How old are you?"

"That has nothing to do with it." He pulled the cover and reached for her hand. "Let's go."

"Hand me my robe." She yawned. "You may come in on me some day and wish you hadn't."

"I intend to wake you up every Christmas I have an opportunity to." He leaned in to kiss her cheek.

"By the way, I told Nan I'm going to Seminary and she said okay."

"Is the world ready for you," she grumbled, following him out the door and down the stairs.

"It will be," he assured her. "I'll post you regularly and come back to Safe Haven when I can."

She sighed. The tree was lit, and every nook and cranny, too, and gifts piled high under the tree.

Nan and Jonathan sat on the sofa waiting. In the back ground, somewhere streaming from the kitchen radio they could hear Christmas carols.

"It's perfect. Just as I remember," Thomas James exclaimed as Elizabeth rolled her eyes. But a smile escaped as she, Nan and Jonathan laughed. "What?" He asked. "Merry Christmas. Right?"

"Jonathan will read the Christmas story this afternoon after dinner, if that's okay with you two, we'll skip it for now. We've got a lot of friends and family coming for dinner so we better keep moving along." Nan patted her husband's knee. "Merry Christmas, Darling. Merry Christmas, Kids."

****

Nan's guests begin to arrive, the food was set on the buffet, except for the beautiful turkey Jonathan would carve and as Elizabeth looked around she saw the people of her heart, Nan and Jonathan and Thomas James, Marge and Lettie, Lettie's two grand daughter's and Joe who seemed to be watching the door. Next was Bobby and Elaine and their three children and Mr. Larson. Almost her heart wanted to be sad, but this was Jesus birthday and like Joe she might be waiting for someone but in her case that one wasn't coming. She prayed Joe would not be disappointed. Grace was said and Jonathan began to carve the turkey as plates were passed and the room became active as they went to the buffet to fill their plates. The door bell rang and Nan said, "I will get it." That's unusual, Elizabeth thought, but she was busy scooping salad into bowl's and delivering them to the table.

Finally everyone was seated and Elizabeth glanced to see who had come in. Her heart lurched. Seated by Joe was Catrin on one side and on the other a young lady she suspected to be his daughter. It was hard to guess her age, anywhere between fifteen and twenty, but it was Catrin sitting by Joe seemed to be a mistake until she saw Derek farther down by his father and then it made sense, Mr. Larson was already seated when Derek arrived. Their eyes met, direct, no signal of remembrance of their history, no indication of past innuendoes of love, just acknowledgement they were present. In contrast, Joe and Derek almost seemed friends. Or, maybe she was on the defensive in all things. For a moment she felt Nan and Jonathan's eyes on her and then their breath of relief that she accepted those invited. She would not contest the right of Nan to ask or her guest receiving. Everyone settled to eating and commenting on Nan's delicious food. Thomas James was in happy heaven with his family and friends. Elizabeth considered, again this was her lot in life to accept whatever came her way and make it work. She closed her eyes, took a deep breath and resolved to do her best.

Bobby spoke up, "You know," he said, "There's a gathering of those who would sing the carols planned for four o'clock this afternoon to meet at City Hall. Everyone's invited."

"Let's do it," she heard Thomas James say, and the murmuring consensus was that all would go.

She made it through the dinner. Serving helped keep her mind busy and she found she could avoid the section where Derek and his father sit which was across the table from Joe, his daughter and Catrin. The three together seemed almost unbelievable, but the girl rose to the occasion, therefore the parents had to.

Once the table was cleared, Lettie's granddaughter's began stacking the dishes in the dishwasher and cleaning the kitchen. Lettie had whispered the girls needed money, was there anything they could do, and their help lightened the load. Somehow Elizabeth and Catrin avoided each other and soon it was time for Jonathan to read the scripture of Christmas and Christ's birth. When he finished reading from the Bible, Jonathan explained, "we all have a Christmas story. In our hearts lives the humble beginning of our life, and as we think of the Keeper of the inn who turned them away because the rooms were taken, the shepherds in the field, and the angels, all wanted to be a part of this thing that was taking place. Some way they knew there was new hope and that hope is still alive today to sustain us and carry us through any circumstance of struggle, disappointment or despair. Through him, our needs are met. They may not be according to our plan, but they are according to God's plan for us. Whatever the need we can take it to him. Remember that and keep Christmas and its promise in your life."

It was time to hand out gifts, rather than open them each person was to take their gift home.

Everyone left, thanking Nan and Jonathan for a lovely gathering and then the house was quiet.

Jonathan was first to come into the room where she sit. "I'm here to find our coats and whatever it takes to stay warm," he explained. "We're going to the caroling event. Are you?"

"No, not this time," she replied. "I'm very thankful for many things, Jonathan. But I think not today."

"Don't fret, Elizabeth. I understand. Losing Em was such a big thing in my life, I thought it was the ultimate loss but there followed many unsettling situations when I had to yield myself to the Lord. I'm not saying you face anything like that, but in knowing you I'm saying whatever you feel is right for You." He started out of the room and turned back. "Do you know what a joy it is for me to know your mother?" She didn't answer. Jonathan smiled. "Thank you for accepting me, Elizabeth."

Chapter 12

She was restless. Maiybe she should have gone with the family to the caroling but being in the group with Catrin and Derek was more than she could handle today. She admitted there was a slight anticipation when she returned to Mosby of seeing Derek again. She wasn't certain if he married or not but a mutual friend who saw Derek occasionally said he was single presently.

No one knew Addison was abusive. She had built his persona through the years embarrassed that she must do that to protect her own and she prayed no one ever knew. When Derek accused her of marrying a man of lesser statue it had taken her by surprise and twist the knife around her heart.

Going to the rack, she put on her coat, pulled a hat over her head and ears and found gloves in the coat pocket. With a second thought she wrapped a heavy afghan around her shoulders and left. She would make her way to the tree house. It seemed fitting to go there today. The road was slippery since there were no tracks and no one had traveled it. Once there she leaned back against the post Derek used to tie the bench to when a gang decide to take it. She smiled, remembering. The gang was a group of ten year olds that wanted to be fierce and feared, but the city police had encouraged their parents to let him keep them in jail overnight, thinking that would probably cure the problem and it did.

"Elizabeth?"

She thought she heard her name. How silly. No one knew she was here.

"Elizabeth."

Bewildered, she turned to stare down the road and closed her eyes to be sure she was seeing someone. It was Derek but if she closed her eyes he would be gone when she opened them but that wasn't his way. Derek stayed. She ran. He stayed because when he was a little boy his mother left first, and then his Daddy; they left him behind and he stayed because that was all he could do.

"Derek."

"I came to apologize."

"You don't have to apologize to me."

"I do. For the first time at the office when I saw you and not expecting you, I said things I shouldn't have, that one about your husband. I'm really sorry. It was that last to know syndrome, You and Bill seemed in cahoots and I didn't like it."

"We've been through this, before."

"Then I was judgmental of you at the Club with what you said to Catrin, even knowing she had probably said something to you in the past."

"Nothing matters, Derek. You can consider it all closed and go your way."

"Go home with me, Elizabeth. Come with me now, while there's still a part of Christmas for us to celebrate together."

She was shocked. It brought her to her feet. "What do you mean? Us celebrate?"

"Is that so far out you can't understand? Have you forgotten what I said to you the other night?"

"I believe you said I must answer you that night or you might ask the first person you met to marry you. I assume you did just that."

"I don't understand. What are you talking about?"

"You and Catrin arriving at my mother's house, together. The ring on her finger. I ran in to her at

Macy's and she enjoyed showing the ring to every woman in there, using your name and gaining laughter in the process. I was the one on the outside. Do you know how that feels?"

He stared at her. "Unbelievable. But yes, I do. Your mother used to make me feel like that."

"I thought so, too. It brought back old memories of Catrin always winning, merely by taunting me, wanting anything I had and that was a childhood thing. I don't want it in my adult years."

"Your mother invited us. Did that upset you, too?"

"I came here to think and be grateful but you know what? Yesterday I drove, trying to figure things out, all the way to a small little park and while I was sitting there I realized it was where you took me that day so many years ago when Catrin found my Dad with Sarah and her little boy."

He crossed the distance and sit on the bench, pulling her down beside him. "I've been there a dozen times trying to figure out what went wrong."

"Now you don't have to and neither do I, I guess I'll return to my practice."

"Where? Chicago?" His anger seemed to dissipate. "Please don't go that far. Give us a chance."

He seemed so disappointed she had to access the conversation. This wasn't Derek. He didn't give a ring to one woman and then talk to another, not the old Derek any way, but then there was the dance."

"Is Catrin wearing an engagement ring?"

"It seems she is."

"Just a yes or no, Derek. Did you give Catrin an engagement ring?"

"Are you crazy?"

"I think maybe I am, to sit here discussing my future in such a way."

"What about mine? I've wasted nearly twenty years waiting for you."

She was so frustrated she wanted to, she didn't know what she wanted. "I'm leaving." She said.

"No, not til we finish this."

"Did you give Catrin an engagement ring?"

"No. I told you I didn't. Joe gave her a ring. They decided to try marriage again because of their daughter." He stared at her, his mind still trying to work through the process of what she thought, in regard to what he knew. "This is the most ridiculous conversation we've ever had. I came to ask you to go home with me and you want to talk about Catrin. I thought you were sick of her shenanigans."

"I am." Suddenly she was cold and her brain felt numb. Derek was making disclaimers of every thing she thought to be true. "You're not engaged to Catrin and you want me to go with you to your home, for no reason other than to be kind and considerate and see if we still like each other?" She couldn't help grinning. There was a feeling in her heart she hadn't experienced in a long time. "I'd love to."

"You would?" Now he eyed her, carefully. "you wouldn't do this to punish me, would you?"

"Whatever do you mean? I thought you ask me to your home because there's privacy there."

"I did, but now I'm wondering if you'll punish me in some way."

Elizabeth began to laugh. "We don't trust each other. After all we've been through. I can't believe it." Suddenly it seemed completely out of character for both of them. She bent over laughing. "we don't trust each other and we don't know what to do. Come on, we'll walk the lane together. Just like old times." She slid, almost falling down. He caught her by the arm. "Thanks."

"No, it's more than that." He pulled her into his arms. "I've been wanting to kiss you since that day in the office. That was so frustrating, you will never know."

"But you have kissed me."

She had not forgotten. She should have being married to Addison but there was something about

Derek, knowing if they were together he wouldn't wander off under the guiles of another female.

She breathed in, peaceful, in relief, she supposed. Derek was kissing her and she was responding. He pulled the afghan around her shoulders and she felt the tickle of a smile move across his face.

"Uh, huh, you are still interested," he said, smug and happy at the same time. "I'm taking you to my house. We will have a fire in the fireplace, pop corn, and sit on the sofa until you have to go home. Twenty years is not a lifetime but it has felt like it."

"You really never married?"

"No," he replied, "but you did."

She felt the accusations. "Are you going to bring it up, again."

He studied her face a moment. She was serious. "No, Lizzie, I promise, I won't." He hooked an arm through hers. "I love you too much for that."

"What's next?" She asked.

He groaned. "Well, next week you come back to the office and help me find whoever named the newest prosthesis." She leaned back to look into his eyes, tilting her head just so.

"Are you kidding me?"

"That I won't do either. I've learned I can't outdo or outwit you. Never could, but I can love you and take care of you like a fine southern gentleman. Are you interested?"

"Yeah, I am and I may know something about your prosthesis. Is it a small device, about so…and…so?" She grinned. "Do they call it an Exemplar?"

"How do you know that?"

"That's what I'm paid to know." She grinned. "Merry Christmas, Derek."

"Merry Christmas, Lizzie." He leaned down to kiss her. "It's going to be a good day, after all."

"Ummm…yes," she agreed. "But in case you haven't noticed, it is going to be night."

****

"Where are the kids," Jonathan asked. "It's kind of quiet without them."

"Tommy was smitten by Joe's daughter. I forget her name… Madeline Grace."

"I'm sure you will hear it enough in the next few days," he laughed. "I didn't know kids could be fun. I thought they were all work and no play. Your two seem to like playing, games and such."

"Yeah," she grinned. "Remember, Tommy is mine by acceptance. He and I hit it right off and love each other."

"Kind of strange with him being your first husband's love child."

"Is that what you call him?" Nancy Ann tilt her head remembering the night she heard Sarah died and left Thomas James without a mother. "I thought, what if that were Elizabeth, could another woman love my daughter and I decided right then I wanted to meet Tommy and we put puzzles together and completely confounded his father." She gave a delightful laugh. "What do you call a family like ours?"

"Knowing you, I call it delightful but I suppose it's like all others people call dysfunctional, though I see nothing dysfunctional about it. Some families can meld together while others choose to stay apart."

"You are a delightful husband, Jonathan. Thank God, I decided I could afford a winter in Florida and there you were behind the pulpit when I went to church on Sunday."

"And here we are enjoying Christmas together. The house is decorated beautifully. There's warmth.

We must pray for those less fortunate, who do not know the Lord and who need necessary things to make life easier. We are so blessed, Nan. I thank God we can understand the true meaning of Christmas, that it's not just gifts and bountiful dinners but that we celebrate God sending His son to earth for us, to die on a cross that we might have salvation. But many do not understand and there lies my heart's concern. To tell the world, we must start right here in our own corner."

"Spoken like a called minister, my love. I certainly never thought I would be a minister's wife."

"God knew, Nan, the way you care about others. That dinner and inviting those with problems in their lives. For a minute I was afraid Elizabeth couldn't handle it, but she is a trouper."

"Yes, she is. She practically became Tommy's mother after Frank's Sarah died."

"Then what capacity did you fill?"

"Just Nan. He named me that very first day. I am so blessed, otherwise I wouldn't have a grandchild, would I?" She gave a content sigh. "What do you suppose Elizabeth and Derek are deciding?"

******

The flame danced its bluish tinged dance of red and gold, the sap in the logs snapping now and then as they sit on the sofa, pulled near enough their feet were warm. Hands entwined, Derek unlaced his fingers and stood, "I'll be right back," he said and left going toward his bedroom. He returned a short time later, with something in his hand. Dropping down on one knee, he took her left hand again.

"Elizabeth," he said, his voice husky. "I've waited what seemed a forever eternity to ask this." She leaned forward to kiss his forehead. "Elizabeth, will you marry me and let us love each other until death parts our life together?" He held the ring in his right hand, ready to slip it on her finger.

Tears ran down her cheeks. "Oh, Derek, yes. Forever into eternity if God grants it. I want to be your wife."

He slipped the ring on her finger as their lips met. "But soon, like next week. Is that all right?"

"It's more than all right."

"I love you, Elizabeth."

"I love you, Derek."

"Merry Christmas," they said together.

The End

Books by Betty Lowrey

PROMISES
SECRETS
FORGIVEN
FORBIDDEN
FORSAKEN
FOREVER
FORGOTTEN
WHEN SOMEBODY LOVES YOU
FOR THE LOVE OF STORMY WEATHER
LOVING YOU ALWAYS
WHEN DREAMS COME TRUE
WHERE THERE'S LOVE
WHEN YOU CALL MY NAME
ENGRAVED ON MY HEART
WHEN MY HEART SINGS
A HEART TWICE BLESSED
FAITH IN SPITE OF THE STORM
BARKLEY
LILY
EMMA
AMANDA
A HEART WAITS FOREVER (2024)

www.ingramcontent.com/pod-product-compliance
Lightning Source LLC
Chambersburg PA
CBHW060534160726
47991CB00001B/313